MINI MAP+GUIDE

LISBON

CONTENTS

EXPERIENCE

NEED TO KNOW

Left: The MAAT by Amanda Levete Architects
Right: The pavement map, Belém

KEY TO MAIN ICONS

- 📍 Map
- 📍 Address/Location
- 📞 Telephone
- 🚆 Train
- Ⓜ Metro
- 🚋 Tram
- 🚡 Funicular
- ⛴ Ferry
- 🚤 Riverboat
- ℹ Visitor information
- 🕐 Open
- 🔒 Closed
- 🌐 Website

MIX
Paper from
responsible sources

FSC
www.fsc.org   FSC™ C018179

Penguin
Random
House

Main Contributors Matthew Hancock,
Mandy Tomlin, Andy Gregory,
Susie Boulton and Sarah McAllster

Design Nidhi Mehra, Priyanka Thakur

Editorial Shikha Kulkarni, Beverly Smart

Indexer Manjari Thakur

Picture Research Sumita Khatwani, Ellen Root

Cartography Suresh Kumar

Jacket Designers Maxine Pedliham, Amy Cox

DTP Narender Kumar, Jason Little, Tanveer Zaidi

Delhi Team Head Malavika Talukder

Art Director Maxine Pedliham

Publishing Director Georgina Dee

Conceived by Priyanka Thakur
and Shikha Kulkarni

Printed and bound in China

Content previously published in DK Eyewitness
Lisbon (2019). This abridged edition first
published in 2020

Published in Great Britain by
Dorling Kindersley Limited
80 Strand, London WC2R ORL

Published in the United States by DK Publishing, 1450
Broadway, Suite 801, New York, NY 10018

19 20 21 22 10 9 8 7 6 5 4 3 2 1

A CIP catalogue record is available
from the British Library.

A catalogue record for this book is
available from the Library of Congress.

ISBN 978-0-2413-9779-4

**The information in this DK Eyewitness
Travel Guide is checked regularly.**
Every effort has been made to ensure this book
is up-to-date at the time of going to press.
However, details such as addresses, opening
hours, prices and travel information, are liable to
change. The publishers cannot accept
responsibility for any consequences arising
from the use of this book, nor for any
material on third-party websites. If you
have any comments, please write to: DK
Eyewitness Travel Guides, Dorling Kindersley,
80 Strand, London WC2R ORL, UK, or email:
travelguides@dk.com.

WELCOME TO
LISBON

Creamy custard tarts and the spine-tingling wail of traditional *fado* music. Steep, winding streets, with incredible views waiting at the top. World-class art, found within renowned museums or along *azulejo*-lined city streets. Whatever your ideal break to Lisbon includes, this DK Eyewitness Mini Map and Guide will prove the perfect travelling companion.

Long lauded for its plentiful sunshine and excellent value, Lisbon's charms run far deeper. As befits one of the world's oldest cities, the capital of Portugal oozes history and tradition. Ancient buildings – from the Moorish to the Manueline – dot its diverse neighbourhoods (many of which can be traversed by jaunty wooden tram), while the brimming galleries of the Museu Nacional de Arte Antiga and the Museu Calouste Gulbenkian Founder's Collection also indicate a rich past. Beyond the city centre, day trips to palace-strewn Sintra or the golden shores of Lisbon's oft-forgotten beaches are within easy reach.

But the city also has a deserved reputation for European cool. Sample the vibrant nightlife of the Bairro Alto and Cais do Sodré districts, or peruse contemporary design collections at the eye-catching Museu de Arte, Arquitetura e Tecnologia (MAAT). While traditional refreshments – think fresh seafood and the country's ubiquitous fortified wine – are still very much a draw, a fast-developing foodie scene and rooftop bars that make the most of Lisbon's spectacular panoramas now offer travellers a slick alternative.

From the jumbled streets of the Alfama to atmospheric Belém and beyond, we've broken Lisbon down into easily navigable chapters, highlighting each area's unmissable sights and unexpected delights. Add insider tips, leisurely walks, a comprehensive fold-out map and a need-to-know section full of expert advice for before and during your trip, and you've got an indispensable guidebook. Enjoy the book, and enjoy Lisbon.

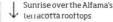

↓ Sunrise over the Alfama's terracotta rooftops

ALFAMA

Lisbon's oldest district, the labyrinthine Alfama tumbles downhill towards the river, hiding tiny bars, secret squares and a traditional way of life amid its narrow streets. This is the birthplace of *fado*, Portugal's mournful style of music, and the neighbourhood still hosts the Feira a Ladra, an authentic, twice-weekly street market packed with everything from postcards to antiques. Some of Lisbon's best viewpoints can also be found in the Alfama, with both the castle's ramparts and the Miradouro de Santa Luzia offering sweeping panoramas over the rest of the city.

CASTELO DE SÃO JORGE

Torre de
Ulisses

📍 W2 🏠 Porta de São Jorge (entrance on Rua de Santa Cruz do Castelo) 🚌 737 🚋 28 🕐 Mar-Oct: 9am-9pm daily; Nov-Feb: 9am-6pm daily (check website for further details) 🌐 castelodesaojorge.pt

Towering above central Lisbon, this Moorish citadel is one of the city's most recognizable landmarks. Though much of the present castle dates from a 1930s restoration, visitors still flock to the top of the hill to seek out traces of the city's history and enjoy the spectacular views laid out below.

Following the recapture of Lisbon from the Moors in 1147, Dom Afonso Henriques transformed their hilltop citadel into the residence of the Portuguese kings. In 1511, Manuel I built a more lavish palace in what is now the Praça do Comércio, and the citadel castle was used variously as a theatre, prison and arms depot. After the 1755 earthquake, the ramparts remained in ruins until 1938, when António Salazar began a complete renovation, rebuilding the "medieval" walls and adding gardens and wildfowl. The castle may not be authentic, but the gardens and the narrow streets of the Santa Cruz district within the walls make a pleasant stroll, and views from the observation terrace are some of the finest in Lisbon. Other attractions on-site include the city's only camera obscura and the Casa do Leão restaurant, built within part of the former royal residence. Book a table for dinner; the restaurant is also open at lunchtime to those with a ticket for the castle.

TORRE DE ULISSES

Named after the Greek hero Ulysses, who supposedly founded Lisbon on his meander home from Troy, this tower contains a camera obscura – a complicated system of lenses and mirrors that projects 360° views of the city onto the walls in real time. Views are weather-dependent; sunny mornings, when the light is soft, yield the clearest images.

The Museu do Castelo, which displays artifacts from the archaeological site and charts the history of the city.

The tangled site of the Castelo São Jorge, packed inside a walled perimeter

Porta de Martim Moniz, a gate named after the knight who gave his life to keep it open for Afonso Henriques' troops in 1147.

An archaeological site containing the ruins of settlements dating from before the original citadel was built.

The 12th-century church of Santa Cruz do Castelo, inside which is a 17th-century statue of St George.

Rua de Santa Cruz do Castelo, a pretty street south of the castle.

Entrance

Porta de São Jorge

→ Afonso Henriques, the first king of Portugal

EXPERIENCE MORE

↑ A bric-a-brac stall at the Feira da Ladra flea market

Feira da Ladra

♀ Y2 **⌂** Campo de Santa Clara **◄** 712 **▭** 28
⌚ 9am–5pm Tue & Sat

The stalls of the so-called "Thieves' Market" have occupied this site on the edge of the Alfama for over a century, laid out under the shade of trees or canopies. As the fame of this flea market has grown, bargains are increasingly hard to find among the mass of bric-a-brac, but a few of the vendors have interesting wrought-iron work, prints and tiles, as well as second-hand clothes. Evidence of Portugal's colonial past is reflected in the stalls selling African statuary, masks and jewellery.

Santa Engrácia

♀ Y2 **⌂** Campo de Santa Clara **◄** 218 854 820
▭ 712 **▭** 28 **⌚** 10am–6pm Tue–Sun (to 5pm Nov–Mar) **⌚** 1 Jan, 25 Apr, Easter Sun, 13 Jun, 24 & 25 Dec

One of Lisbon's most striking landmarks, the soaring dome of Santa Engrácia (officially known as Panteão Nacional) punctuates the skyline in the east of the city. The original church collapsed in a storm in 1681. The first stone of the new Baroque monument, laid in 1682, marked the beginning of a 284-year saga that led to the invention of a saying

> **⊘ GREAT VIEW**
> **Miradouro de Santa Luzia**
>
> The terrace by the church of Santa Luzia provides a sweeping view over the Alfama and the Tagus river. Landmarks, from left to right, are the cupola of Santa Engrácia, the church of Santo Estêvão and the white towers of São Miguel. While tourists admire the views, old men play cards under the bougainvillea-clad pergola.

that a Santa Engrácia job was never done. The church was not completed until 1966.

The interior is paved with coloured marble and crowned by a giant cupola. As the National Pantheon, it houses cenotaphs of Portuguese heroes, such as Vasco da Gama and Afonso de Albuquerque, Viceroy of India (1502–15) on the left, and on the right Henry the Navigator. More contemporary tombs include that of the *fadista* Amália Rodrigues. A lift up to the dome offers a magnificent 360-degree panorama of the city.

São Vicente de Fora

📍 Y2 🏛 Largo de São Vicente 📞 218 885 652 🚌 712, 734 🚃 28 🕐 9am–5pm Tue–Sat, 9–11am Sun; museum: 10am–5pm Tue–Sun 🚫 Public hols

St Vincent was proclaimed Lisbon's patron saint in 1173, when his relics were transferred from the Algarve to a church on this site outside *(fora)* the city walls. Designed by the Italian architect Filippo Terzi, and completed in 1627, the sober off-white façade is in Italian Renaissance style, with towers either side and three arches leading to the entrance hall. Statues of saints Augustine, Vincent and Sebastian can be seen over the entrance.

The adjoining former Augustinian monastery, reached via the nave, retains its 16th-century cistern and vestiges of the former cloister, but it is visited mainly for its 18th-century *azulejos*. Among the panels in the entrance hall off the first cloister there are lively, though historically inaccurate, tile scenes of Afonso Henriques attacking Lisbon and Santarém.

Deeper into the monastery, floral designs and cherubs illustrate the fables of La Fontaine. A passageway leads behind the church to the old refectory, transformed into the Bragança Pantheon in 1885. The stone sarcophagi of almost every king and queen are here, from João IV, who died in 1656, to Manuel II, last king of Portugal. Only Maria I and Pedro IV are not buried here. A stone mourner kneels at the tomb of Carlos I and his son Luís Felipe, assassinated in Praça do Comércio in 1908. The church now operates as a museum, with access to the Bragança Pantheon.

↓ Intricate marble inlays adorning São Vicente de Fora

Museu Militar

📍 Y3 🏛 Largo do Museu da Artilharia 🚌 728, 735, 759 🚋 28 🕙 10am-5pm Tue-Sun 🚫 Public hols 🌐 exercito.pt

Located on the site of a 16th-century cannon foundry and arms depot, visits here begin in the Vasco da Gama Room, with cannons and modern murals depicting the discovery of the sea route to India. The Salas da Grande Guerra display exhibits related to World War I. Other rooms focus on the evolution of weapons in Portugal, from flints to spears to rifles. The courtyard, flanked by cannons, tells the story of Portugal in tiled panels, from the Christian reconquest to World War I. The Portuguese artillery section displays the wagon used to transport the triumphal arch to Rua Augusta.

Casa dos Bicos

📍 W4 🏛 Rua dos Bacalhoeiros 10 📞 218 802040 🚌 728, 735, 759 🚋 15, 25 🕙 10am-6pm Mon-Sat

Faced with diamond-shaped stones (bicos), Casa dos Bicos (House of Spikes) looks rather conspicuous among all the other buildings in the Alfama area. It was built in 1523 for Brás de Albuquerque, illegitimate son of Afonso, Viceroy of India and conqueror of Goa and Malacca. The façade is an adaptation of a style that was popular across Europe during the 16th century. The top two storeys, ruined in the earthquake of 1755, were restored in the 1980s, recreating the original from old views of Lisbon in tile panels and engravings. In the interim the building was used for salting fish (Rua dos Bacalhoeiros means "street of the cod fishermen").

Following an extensive renovation in the 20th century, Casa dos Bicos now plays host to the headquarters of the José Saramago Foundation. It is also home to a permanent exhibition dedicated to the life and works of this Nobel Prize-winning author, who died in 2010. A variety of cultural events often

→ Street café in front of the 16th-century Casa dos Bicos

← Monumental portico at the entrance to the Museu Militar

take place here; these include concerts, plays and book releases, along with a range of seminars, debates and lively talks.

Museu de Artes Decorativas

📍 X3 🏛 Largo das Portas do Sol 2 🚌 737 🚋 12, 28 🕙 10am–5pm Wed–Mon 📅 1 Jan, 1 May, 25 Dec 🌐 fress.pt

Also known as the Ricardo do Espírito Santo Silva Foundation, the museum was set up in 1953 to preserve the traditions and increase public awareness of the Portuguese decorative arts. The foundation was named after a banker who bought the 17th-century Palácio Azurara in 1947 to house his fine collection of furniture, textiles, silver and ceramics. Among the

17th- and 18th-century antiques displayed in this handsome four-storey mansion are many fine pieces in exotic woods, including an 18th-century rosewood backgammon and chess table. Also of note are the collections of 18th-century silver and Chinese porcelain, and hand-embroidered wool carpets from Arraiolos.

The spacious rooms still retain some original ceilings and *azulejo* panels.

In the adjoining building are workshops where artisans preserve the techniques of cabinet-making, gilding, book-binding, wood-carving and other traditional crafts. Temporary exhibitions, lectures and concerts are also held in the museum.

↑ Ornate carriage on display at Museu de Artes Decorativas

EAT

Chapitô à Mesa

For a meal with a view, the terrace here has jaw-dropping vistas.

 W3 ⌂ Costa do Castelo 7 ☎ 218 867 734

€€€

A Baiuca

This tiny *tasca* has a good menu but even better *fado vadio* (amateur *fado*).

 X3 ⌂ Rua de São Miguel 20 ☎ 218 867 284 🕘 Tue & Wed

€€€

Cantina Zé Avillez

Sample tasty food by one of Lisbon's top chefs at this tiled restaurant.

 W4 ⌂ Rua dos Arameiros 15 ⓦ cantinazeavillez.pt

€€€

Museu do Aljube – Resistência e Liberdade

📍 W4 ⌂ Rua Augusta Rosa 42 🕘 10am-6pm Tue-Sat 🕘 1 Jan, 1 May, 25 Dec ⓦ museudo aljube.pt

This fascinating museum was once used by António Salazar – who ruled Portugal as a dictator from 1926 until the revolution of 1974 – to imprison his political opponents. It is dedicated to those who were pre-pared to fight for democracy, both in Portugal and in its former colonies. Three floors are filled with evocative photos, posters and radio broadcasts, with labelling in English. There are also harrowing personal accounts from people who were incarcerated and often tortured for views that were considered contrary to those of the state; many of these inmates were later deported to Madeira or the Azores. Their cramped, windowless cells can still be visited.

→

Lisbon's colourful skyline seen from the Miradouro da Graça viewpoint

The basement houses archaeological finds from beneath the building, which date back to Moorish times, while the top-floor café offers fine views over the river.

Museu do Fado

📍 Y3 🏠 Largo do Chafariz de Dentro 1
🚌 728, 735, 759, 794
🕐 10am-6pm Tue-Sun
🌐 museudofado.pt

Alfama is considered the true home of *fado*

and this museum portrays the influence that this ever-popular and intensely heartfelt genre of music has had on the city over the past two centuries. A permanent display traces the genre's history from its origins in the early 19th century to the present day, from Maria Severa, the first *fado* diva, to more contemporary singers like Amália Rodrigues and Mariza. Regular

↑ José Malhoa's *O Fado*, a haunting portrait hanging at the Museu do Fado

temporary exhibitions take place during the year on a range of musical themes, along with the occasional live *fado* concert.

GREAT VIEW
Miradouro da Graça

North of Alfama, the suburb of Graça is visited chiefly for the vistas from its *miradouro* (viewpoint). The panorama of rooftops and skyscrapers is less spectacular than the view from the Castelo de Sao Jorge, but it is a popular spot, particularly in the early evenings, when couples sit at café tables under the pines.

Santo António da Sé

📍W4 🏛Largo Santo António da Sé, 24
📞218 869 145 🚌737
🚋12, 28 🕐8am-7pm daily (to 8pm Sat & Sun); Museu Antoniano: 10am-6pm Tue-Sun

The popular little church of Santo António allegedly stands on the site of the house in which St Anthony was born. The crypt, reached via the tiled sacristy on the left of the church, is all that remains of the original church destroyed by the earthquake of 1755. Work began on the new church in 1757 headed by Mateus Vicente, architect of the Basílica da Estrela, and was partially funded by donations collected by local children with the cry "a small coin for St Anthony".

Even today the floor of the tiny chapel in the crypt is strewn with euros and the walls are scrawled with devotional messages from worshippers.

The church's façade blends the undulating curves of the Baroque style with Neo-Classical Ionic columns on either side of the main portal. Inside, on the way down to the crypt, a modern *azulejo* panel commemorates the visit of Pope John Paul II in 1982. In 1995 the church was given a facelift for the saint's eighth centenary. It is traditional for young couples to visit the church on their wedding day and leave flowers for St Anthony, who is believed to bring good luck to new marriages.

Next door, in the building thought to be

↑ The impressive Baroque façade of Santo António da Sé

where St Anthony was born, the small Museu Antoniano houses artifacts relating to the saint, along with gold- and silverware that used to decorate the church. The most charming exhibit is a 17th-century tiled panel of St Anthony preaching to the fish.

SANTO ANTÓNIO (C 1195-1231)

The best-loved saint of the Lisboetas is St Antony of Padua. Although born and raised in Lisbon, he spent the last months of his life in Padua, Italy. St Anthony joined the Franciscan Order in 1220, impressed by some crusading friars he had met at Coimbra. The friar was a learned and passionate preacher, known for his devotion to the poor and his ability to convert heretics. Many statues and paintings of St Anthony depict him carrying the infant Jesus on a book, while others show him preaching to fish, as St Francis preached to birds. In 1934 Pope Pius XI declared St Anthony a patron saint of Portugal.

Sé

📍W4 🏛Largo da Sé
📞218 866 752 🚌737
🚋12, 28 🕐9am-7pm daily (to 5pm Mon & Sun); treasury: 10am-5pm Mon-Sat

In 1150, three years after Afonso Henriques recaptured Lisbon from the Moors, he built a cathedral for the first bishop of Lisbon, the English Crusader Gilbert of Hastings, on the site of the old mosque. Sé is short for Sede Episcopal, the seat (or see) of a bishop. Devastated by three earth tremors in the 14th century, as well as the earthquake of 1755, and renovated over the centuries, the cathedral you see today blends a variety of architectural styles. The façade, with twin castellated bell towers and a splendid rose window, retains its solid Romanesque aspect. The gloomy interior is simple and austere, and little remains of the embellishment lavished upon it by King João V in the first half of the 18th century. Beyond the renovated Romanesque nave, the ambulatory has nine Gothic chapels.

The Capela de Santo Ildefonso contains the 14th-century sarcophagi of Lopo Fernandes Pacheco, companion in arms to King Afonso IV, and his wife, Maria Vilalobos. The bearded figure of the nobleman, who is holding a sword in his hand, and his wife, clutching a prayer book, are carved onto the tombs with their dogs sitting faithfully at their feet. In the adjacent chancel are the tombs of Afonso IV and his wife, Dona Beatriz.

The Gothic cloister (due to reopen in 2020 after a major renovation) has elegant double arches with some finely carved capitals. One of the chapels is still fitted with its 13th-century wrought-iron gate. Ongoing archaeological excavations in the cloister have unearthed various Roman and other remains. To the left of the cathedral entrance the Franciscan chapel contains the font where St Anthony was baptized in 1195 and is decorated with a tiled scene of him preaching to the fish. The adjacent chapel contains a Baroque Nativity scene made of cork, wood and terracotta by Machado de Castro (1766).

The treasury is at the top of the staircase on the right. It houses silver, ecclesiastical robes, statuary, illustrated manuscripts and a few relics associated with St Vincent, which were transferred to Lisbon from Cabo de São Vicente in southern Portugal in 1173. Legend has it that two sacred ravens kept a vigil over the boat that transported the relics. The ravens and the boat became a symbol of the city of Lisbon, still very much in use today. It is also said that the ravens' descendants used to dwell in the cloisters of the cathedral.

↓ Interior of the
↓ city's cathedral

A SHORT WALK
ALFAMA

Distance 600 m (0.4 miles) **Nearest station** Graça
bus stop **Time** 15 minutes

A fascinating quarter at any time of day, the Alfama comes to life in the late afternoon and early evening; time your walk for this hour, when the locals emerge at their doorways and the small taverns start to fill. Given the steep streets and steps of the neighbourhood, the least strenuous approach is to start at the top and work your way down. A wander through the maze of winding alleyways will reveal picturesque corners and crumbling churches, plus panoramic views from shady terraces, such as the Miradouro de Santa Luzia. A new generation of younger residents has also resulted in a small number of trendy shops and bars.

Statue of St Vincent

Largo das Portas do Sol, on the east side of the Santa Luzia church, with its own terrace viewpoint.

START

Museu de Artes Decorativas, a furniture and arts museum established in a 17th-century palácio by the banker Ricardo do Espírito Santo Silva.

The church of Santa Luzia, with 18th-century blue-and-white azulejo panels on its south wall.

Miradouro de Santa Luzia, a pleasant place to take in the view from the bougainvillea-clad terrace.

0 metres   25   **N**
0 yards   25

Beco das Cruzes is a steep cobbled
street, above which locals often
string their washing between the
tightly packed houses.

Restaurants,
hidden in a
labyrinth of
alleyways,
spill out onto
open-air patios.

The church of
Nossa Senhora dos
Remédios, whose
pinnacled Manueline
portal is all that
remains of the
original building.

Locator Map

BECO DAS CRUZES

RUA DE SÃO MIGUEL

BECO DO MEXIAS

LARGO DO
CHAFARIZ DE
DENTRO

BECO DO POCINHO

RUA DE SÃO PEDRO

FINISH

Rua de São Pedro,
where a lively
early-morning
fish market is
held daily.

São Miguel was rebuilt
after the 1755 earthquake,
although it retains a few
earlier features.

Largo do Chafariz de
Dentro, a square named
after the 17th-century
fountain (chafariz) that
was originally placed
within (dentro) rather
than outside the 14th-
century city walls.

The wide Rua Augusta cutting through Lisbon's Baixa district

BAIXA AND AVENIDA

The Baixa (lower town) is the heart of the city, comprising a grid of streets dotted with shops, cafés and boutiques, and culminating in the wide, waterfront Praça do Comércio. Running through the centre of the district is the pedestrianized Rua Augusta, where throngs of visitors and locals alike gather to shop, graze and gossip. Also in this area is the imposing Avenida da Liberdade, a wide avenue lined with Art Deco buildings that stretches all the way to Parque Eduardo VII.

PRAÇA DO COMÉRCIO

📍N7 🚌711, 714, 759, 794 & many other routes 🚊15, 18, 25

The beautiful riverfront Praça do Comércio is a vast square with shady arcades on three sides and the wide expanse of the Tagus lapping at its southern edge. It was the centrepiece of the Marquês de Pombal's post-earthquake redesign of the city, and today remains a lively gathering place that hosts cultural events and festivals throughout the year.

Known to locals as *Terreiro do Paço* (Palace Square), this huge open space was the site of the royal palace for 400 years. Manuel I transferred the royal residence from Castelo de São Jorge to this more convenient spot by the river in 1511. When the original palace was destroyed in the 1755 earthquake, Pombal housed the new palace in spacious arcaded buildings around three sides of the square. On the fourth side, grand marble steps stretch down to the water's edge.

Highlights of the square include a huge bronze statue of King José I, the impressive Arco da Rua Augusta on the north side and the Lisbon Story Centre, an interactive museum exploring events in the city's history.

HISTORY IN THE MAKING

The Praça do Comércio has been the scene of major events throughout Lisbon's history. On 1 February 1908, King Carlos and his son Luís Felipe were assassinated as they passed through the square, an event that eventually led to the abolition of the monarchy and declaration of the Republic two years later. Then in 1974, the square saw the first uprising of the Armed Forces Movement, whose soldiers – sporting carnations in their rifles – overthrew the Caetano regime in a bloodless revolution.

Bustling Praça do Comércio, dominated by a huge statue of King José I ↓

Locals on the square's stone steps leading down to the wide Tagus river

↑ Museum-goers take in an unusual exhibit at the Lisbon Story Centre

ELEVADOR DE SANTA JUSTA

📍 N6 🏠 Rua de Santa Justa and Largo do Carmo 📞 213 613 000 🕐 7:30am-9:30pm daily (to 11pm May-Sep)

Sandwiched between pale stone buildings, this arresting iron structure is a vertical link between Lisbon's lowest and highest neighbourhoods. A platform at the top provides spectacular city views.

Also known as the Elevador do Carmo, this Neo-Gothic lift was built at the turn of the 20th century by French architect Raoul Mesnier du Ponsard, a student of Alexandre Gustave Eiffel. Made of iron and embellished with filigree, it is one of the more eccentric features of the Baixa. The ticket office is located at the foot of the lift, and from here passengers can travel up and down inside the tower in one of two smart, wood-panelled cabins with brass fittings. At the top is a walkway linking the Baixa with Largo do Carmo in the Bairro Alto, 32 m (105 ft) above. The apex of the tower, reached via an extremely tight spiral stairway, is given over to a viewing gallery. This high vantage point commands splendid views of Rossio, the Baixa, the castle on the opposite hill, the river and the nearby ruins of the Carmo church. The fire that gutted the Chiado district was extinguished close to the lift.

↑ Steps leading up to the impressive Elevador de Santa Justa

A stunning panorama of the Baixa's grid pattern can be seen from the platform.

Filigree motifs decorate the wrought-iron shaft.

↑ The ornate lift shaft and top-level walkway

← Lisbon's historic centre unfurling beneath the viewing gallery at the top of the lift

 INSIDER TIP
Upwardly Mobile

The Santa Justa lift is technically part of Lisbon's public transport system – and therefore a ride is covered by the 24-hour public transport tickets that can be purchased from any metro station.

← Shaded path descending among exotic foliage, Jardim Botânico

on botany, zoology, anthropology, geology and palaeontology, as well as hosting temporary exhibitions on themes such as dinosaurs.

The museum also exhibits scientific instruments dating from the 16th to the 20th century and holds popular, child-friendly programmes that demonstrate basic scientific principles.

Rua Augusta

Q N7   🚌 711, 714, 732, 736, 759 & many other routes   Ⓜ Baixa-Chiado

A lively pedestrianized street decorated with mosaic pavements and lined with boutiques and cafés, Rua Augusta is the main tourist thoroughfare and the smartest in the Baixa. Street performers provide entertainment, while vendors sell souvenirs. The triumphal Arco da Rua Augusta, built to commemorate the city's recovery from the earthquake, was completed only in 1873. There are great views from the top of the arch, which is accessed by an elevator.

EXPERIENCE MORE

Jardim Botânico

Q L5   🏠 Rua da Escola Politécnica 58-60   🚌 758   Ⓜ Rato   🕐 Gardens: 9am–8pm daily (to 5pm Oct–Mar); MUHNAC: 10am–5pm Tue–Fri, 11am–6pm Sat & Sun   🚫 Public hols   🌐 museus.ulisboa.pt

This complex comprises a museum and a 4 ha (10 acres) of gardens. The botanical gardens are well kept, and it is worth paying the entrance fee to wander among the exotic trees and dense paths as the gardens descend from the main entrance towards Rua da Alegria. A magnificent, verdant avenue of lofty palms connects the two levels.

The Museu Nacional de História Natural e da Ciência, or MUHNAC (National Museum of Natural History and Science), has collections

The other main thoroughfares of the Baixa are Rua da Prata (silversmiths' street) and Rua do Ouro or Rua Áurea (goldsmiths' street). Cutting across these main streets are smaller streets that give glimpses up to the Bairro Alto to the west and Castelo de São Jorge to the east. Many streets retain shops that gave them their name: jewellers in Rua da Prata and Rua do Ouro and banks in Rua do Comércio.

In the heart of the Baixa is a small section of the Roman baths, located within the Banco Comercial Português in Rua dos Correeiros. The ruins and mosaics can be seen from the street window at the rear side of the bank; alternatively you can book ahead to visit the "museum" on 211 131 681.

Rossio
📍N6 🚍709, 711, 736 & many other routes
Ⓜ Rossio
Formally called Praça Dom Pedro IV, this large square has been Lisbon's nerve centre for six

centuries: the stage of bullfights, festivals, military parades and gruesome *autos da fé* (acts of faith). The sober Pombaline buildings are now occupied by shops and cafés. Centre stage is a statue of Dom Pedro IV, the first emperor of independent Brazil.

In the mid-19th century, the square was paved with wave-patterned mosaics that gave it the nickname of "Rolling Motion Square". The grey and white stone cubes were the first such designs to decorate the city's pavements.

On the north side of Rossio is the Teatro Nacional Dona Maria II, named after Dom Pedro's daughter. The

Neo-Classical structure was built in the 1840s by the Italian architect Fortunato Lodi. The interior was destroyed by fire in 1964 and reconstructed in the 1970s. Atop the pediment is Gil Vicente (1465–1536), the founder of Portuguese theatre.

Café Nicola on the west side of the square was a favourite meeting place among writers, including the poet Manuel du Bocage (1765–1805), who was notorious for his satires.

Did You Know?

Rossio is home to a public mirror engraved with the words "correct your tie's knot here".

→

Rossio's dramatic central fountain at sunset

Núcleo Arqueológico

⚲ N7 ⌂ Rua dos Correeiros 21 ☎ 211 131 004 ⊙ 10am-noon, 2-5pm Mon-Sat

Late-20th-century renovation works on this site uncovered archaeological finds, many dating back over 2,500 years. These have been preserved, often under glass flooring, and today can be visited in situ as part of a free and interesting guided tour. The cramped underground walkways provide a fascinating insight into Lisbon's history, from pre-Roman times to the 18th century. Displays range from the remains of Roman fish-preserving tanks to wooden pillars used to prop up Baixa's buildings when it was rebuilt on waterlogged land after the earthquake of 1755.

Casa Museu Medeiros e Almeida

⚲ L5 ⌂ Rua Rosa Araújo 41 ⊙ 10am-5pm Mon-Sat �W casamuseumedeirose almeida.pt

This little-known museum off the Avenida is in the former home of António Medeiros e Almeida, an industrialist who amassed an astonishing collection of international arts and crafts before bequeathing it to the nation in the 1970s.

Today the collection sprawls across 27 galleries – housed partly in Medeiros e Almeida's 19th-century mansion and partly in a modern wing. It includes paintings by Rubens, Pieter Bruegel II and Jacob Huysman, with a self-portrait by Rembrandt as one of the highlights.

Other notable items include a tea set that belonged to Napoleon, some of the earliest Chinese porcelain to reach Europe and a collection of ornate watches and clocks.

Avenida da Liberdade

⚲ M5 ⬛ 709, 711, 736 & many other routes ⓜ Restauradores, Avenida

After the earthquake of 1755, the Marquês de Pombal created the Passeio Público (public promenade) in the area now occupied by the lower part of Avenida da Liberdade and Praça dos Restauradores. Despite its name, enjoyment of the park was restricted to Lisbon's high society and walls and gates ensured the exclusion of the lower classes. In 1821, when the Liberals came to power, the barriers were pulled down and the Avenida and square became open to all.

The Avenida da Liberdade you see today was built in 1879–82 to replicate the sophistication and style of the Champs-Elysées in Paris. The wide tree-lined avenue became a focus for pageants, festivities and demonstrations. A war memorial stands as a tribute to those who died in World War I. The avenue still retains a certain elegance, with fountains and café tables shaded by trees; however, it no longer makes for a peaceful stroll. The once majestic thoroughfare, 90 m (295 ft) wide and decorated with abstract pavement patterns, is now divided by seven lanes of traffic linking Praça dos Restauradores and Praça Marquês de Pombal to the north. Many of the Art Nouveau façades have given way to modern ones occupied by offices, hotels or shopping complexes, though some of the original mansions have been preserved. Look out for the Neo-Classical Tivoli cinema at No 188, with an original 1920s kiosk outside, and Casa

Lambertini with its colourful mosaic decoration at No 166.

Praça dos Restauradores

🅠 M6 🚌 709, 711, 736 & many other routes
Ⓜ Restauradores

This square, distinguished by its soaring obelisk erected in 1886, commemorates Portugal's liberation from the Spanish yoke in 1640. The bronze figures on the pedestal depict Victory, holding a palm and a crown, and Freedom. The names and dates that are inscribed on the sides of the obelisk are those of the battles of the War of Restoration.

On the west side, the Palácio Foz now houses a tourist office and other businesses. It was built by Francesco Savario Fabri in 1755–77 for the Marquês de Castelo-Melhor and renamed after the Marquês de Foz, who lived here in the 19th century. The smart Avenida Palace Hotel, on the southwest side of the square, was designed by José Luís Monteiro (1848–1942), who also built Rossio railway station.

→

The soaring obelisk dominating Praça dos Restauradores

Museu da Sociedade de Geografia

Q M5 **A** Rua das Portas de Santo Antão 100 **C** 213 425 401 **B** 709, 711, 736 **M** Restauradores **O** 11am–12:45pm, 2–4:45pm Mon–Fri

This museum houses an idiosyncratic ethnographical collection brought back from Portugal's former colonies. On display are circumcision masks from Guinea Bissau, musical instruments and snake spears. From Angola there are neck rests to sustain coiffures and the original *padrão* – the pillar erected by the Portuguese in 1482 to mark their sovereignty over the colony.

Nossa Senhora da Conceição Velha

Q N7 **A** Rua da Alfândega **C** 218 870 202 **B** 759, 794 **T** 18, 25 **O** 10am–2pm, 3–6pm daily

The elaborate Manueline doorway of the church is the only surviving feature from the original 16th-century Nossa Senhora da Misericórdia, which stood here until the 1755 earthquake. The portal is decorated with a profusion of Manueline detail, including angels, beasts, flowers and the cross of the Order of Christ. In the tympanum, the Virgin Mary spreads her protective mantle over various contemporary figures. These include Pope Leo X, Manuel I and his sister, Queen Leonor,

> **Q HIDDEN GEM**
> **Elevador da Lavra**
>
> Seek out the Elevador da Lavra, one of the city's lesser-known street lifts located at the end of Largo da Anunciada. Dating back to 1884, it climbs up to the pretty Jardim do Torel gardens.

widow of João II. It was Leonor who founded the original Misericórdia (alms house) on the site of a former synagogue.

MUDE (Museu do Design e da Moda)

Q N7 **A** Rua Augusta 24 **O** 10am–6pm Tue–Sun (closed for renovation, check website for updates) **W** mude.pt

Anyone with an interest in design or fashion will want to linger at this tremendous collection of 20th-century classics from around the world, which traces the evolution of design from the 1930s onwards. The bulk of the pieces on display are from the private collection of Francisco Capelo, which

MUDE, with the Arco da Rua Augusta in the background

the wealthy economist bequeathed to the state in 2003.

Exhibits are overhauled regularly, but usually feature the likes of "Marilyn's lips" (Bocca's iconic mouth-shaped sofa), furniture by Philippe Starck or Charles and Ray Eames, and wonderful haute couture from Vivienne Westwood, Jean-Paul Gaultier and Alexander McQueen.

Praça da Figueira
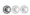 N6 🚌 714, 759, 760 & many other routes 🚋 12, 15 Ⓜ Rossio

Before the 1755 earthquake, the square next to Rossio was the site of the Hospital de Todos-os-Santos (All Saints). In Pombal's new design for the Baixa, the square took on the role of the city's central marketplace. In 1885 a covered market was built, but this was pulled down in the 1950s. Today, the four-storey buildings are given over to hotels, shops and cafés and the square is no longer a marketplace. Perhaps its most eye-catching feature is the multitude of pigeons that perch on the pedestal supporting Leopoldo de Almeida's bronze equestrian statue of João I, erected in 1971.

EAT

Bonjardim, Rei dos Frangos
On a side street, this is the ideal place to sample Portugal's spit-roast chicken – with or without fiery piri-piri sauce.

 M6 🏠 Travessa de Santo Antão 11-18 📞 213 424 389 🕐 Wed in winter

€€€

Cervejaria Ribadouro
Set in a striking 1920s building, this bustling restaurant and brewery does a strong line in fresh seafood.

📍 M5 🏠 Avenida da Liberdade 155 🌐 cervejariaribadouro.pt

€€€

Confeitaria Nacional
This historic café opened in 1829 and still serves a tempting array of pastries, teas and strong coffee.

📍 N6 🏠 Praça da Figueira 18 📞 213 424 470

€€€

→

Equestrian statue of João I standing in Praça da Figueira

A SHORT WALK
RESTAURADORES

Distance 1.3 km (0.8 miles) **Nearest station** Restauradores metro **Time** 20 minutes

This is the busiest part of Lisbon, especially the central squares of Rossio and Praça da Figueira. Totally rebuilt after the earthquake of 1755, the area was one of Europe's first examples of town planning. Stroll the wide streets to admire the large Neo-Classical buildings, before absorbing more of the atmosphere and surroundings from one of the bustling pavement cafés. Nearby Rua das Portas de Santo Antão, a pedestrianized street where restaurants display tanks of live lobsters, allows for a more leisurely pace.

The Elevador da Glória funicular goes up the hill towards the Bairro Alto, as far as the Miradouro de São Pedro de Alcântara.

Built by Italian architect Francesco Fabri, the magnificent 18th-century Palácio Foz is now home to a tourist office.

This large tree- and café-lined square was named after the soldiers who gave their lives during the War of Restoration.

Restauradores

The Neo-Manueline Rossio Station boasts an eye-catching façade featuring two Moorish-style horseshoe arches.

START

PRAÇA DOS RESTAURADORES

FINISH

RUA DA

T. DE SA

← The serene Neo-Moorish patio at Casa do Alentejo

Museu da Sociedade de Geografia, a museum with an extensive collection of items brought back from Portugal's former colonies.

Casa do Alentejo, a spectacularly restored Alentejan restaurant, features a Neo-Moorish patio and fountain.

Named after a 15th-century gate that once stood here, lively Rua das Portas de Santo Antão is now filled with excellent seafood restaurants.

Locator Map

BAIXA AND
AVENIDA

0 metres   50
0 yards   50
N ↑

PORTAS DE SANTO ANTÃO

LARGO DO REGEDOR

LARGO DE SÃO DOMINGOS

PRAÇA DOM JOÃO DA CÂMARA

ROSSIO (PRAÇA DOM PEDRO IV)

RUA 10 DE DEZEMBRO

Teatro Nacional Dona Maria II

Church of São Domingos

Rossio

Praça da Figueira was designed as the city's main marketplace in Pombal's reconstruction of the area.

PRAÇA DA FIGUEIRA

Rossio

Café Nicola

This attractively paved square is home to cafés, pastelarias and the National Theatre on its north side.

Locals enjoying dinner outside in Bairro Alto's Calçada do Duque

BAIRRO ALTO AND ESTRELA

The Bairro Alto is Lisbon's nightlife district. By day it's relatively tranquil, but at night the neighbourhood comes alive with restaurants, cafés and bars that spill revellers out into the streets until the early hours. In Cais do Sodré you'll find the literally named Pink Street: once Lisbon's red light district, but now populated with stylish cocktail bars and clubs. The area offers culture, too, from Estrela's grand domed basilica to the impressive Museu Nacional de Arte Antiga in Lapa, home of Portugal's national art collection.

MUSEU NACIONAL DE ARTE ANTIGA

📍 J8 🏠 Rua das Janelas Verdes 🚌 713, 714, 727 🚋 15, 18 🕐 10am–6pm Tue–Sun 🚫 1 Jan, Easter, 1 May, 25 Dec 🌐 museudearteantiga.pt

Portugal's national art collection is housed in a lemon-yellow 17th-century palace, originally built for the counts of Alvor. Among the exhibits are more state-designated "national treasures" than anywhere else in the country.

Inaugurated in 1884, the museum is known locally as the Museu das Janelas Verdes, a nod to the former green windows of the palace. In 1940, an annexe (including the main façade) was built on the site of the St Albert Carmelite monastery, which was partially demolished between 1910 and 1920. All that survived was a chapel, now integrated into the museum (although currently closed for restoration). After an afternoon's culture, the magnificent garden overlooking the Tagus offers an oasis of calm, plus an adjoining restaurant that serves delicious coffee and pastries. The museum's collection emphasizes Portuguese works, as well as paintings, artifacts and an extensive collection of jewellery from around the world. Highlights of the permanent collection include the exquisite 16th-century Namban screens, which depict contemporary Japanese trade with Portugal.

→

The museum's walls and pretty gardens, within which sits a café (inset)

Visitors admire *The Temptation of St Anthony*, a depiction of spiritual torment by the Dutch master of fantasy, Hieronymus Bosch 3 (1450–1516)

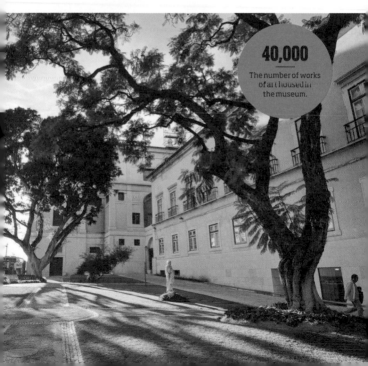

40,000

The number of works of art housed in the museum.

The museum's bright, wide galleries lined with priceless paintings ↑

Exploring the Collections

The museum has the largest collection of paintings in Portugal, including an extensive treasury of early religious works by Portuguese artists. The majority of exhibits came from convents and monasteries following the suppression of religious orders in 1834. There are also wide-ranging displays of sculpture, silverware, porcelain and applied arts, giving an overview of Portuguese art from the Middle Ages to the 19th century, complemented by fine European and Eastern pieces. The theme of the Discoveries is ever-present, illustrating Portugal's links with Brazil, Africa, India, China and Japan.

Did You Know?

Hieronymus Bosch never dated his works, so we can't be exactly sure when they were painted.

← Visitors admiring the São Vicente de Fora polyptych, one of the museum's most important pieces

↑ Gallery of Portuguese painting and sculpture with exhibits on display

TOP 5 **UNMISSABLE EXHIBITS**

Ivory Salt Cellar
Portuguese dignitaries are carved in ivory on this 16th-century West African salt shaker.

The Chapel of St Albert
Admire the Baroque interior, covered in blue-and-white azulejos.

Faïence Violin
Portraits of Italian composers decorate this ceramic piece.

Salomé
Lucus Cranach the Elder's study of virtue or seductive perversion.

The Temptations of St Anthony
A fantastical oil-on-oak triptych.

 Top Collections

European Art

Paintings by European artists, dating from the 14th to the 19th century, hang chronologically on the ground floor. Most of the works in this section were donated from private collections, contributing to the great diversity of works on display. Among the most notable works are *Salomé* by Lucus Cranach the Elder (1472-1553) and *The Temptation of St Anthony* by Hieronymus Bosch (1450-1516).

Portuguese Painting and Sculpture

Many of the earliest works of art are by the Portuguese primitive painters, who were influenced by a Flemish trend of realistic detail. Thought to be by Nuno Gonçalves, the *São Vicente de Fora* polyptych, which shows religious, as well as contemporary figures, is an invaluable historical and social document. The sculpture collection includes many Gothic polychrome stone and wood statues.

Portuguese and Chinese Ceramics

The collection of Chinese porcelain and Portuguese faïence showcases the reciprocal influence between Far Eastern and Portuguese potters. From the 16th century, Portuguese ceramics show a marked influence of Ming, and conversely, Chinese pieces bear Portuguese motifs such as coats of arms. By the mid 18th century, an increasingly personalized, European style emerged among Portuguese potters, using popular, rustic designs.

Asian and African Art

The collection of ivories and furniture, with their European motifs, further illustrates the reciprocal influences of Portugal and her colonies. The 16th-century vogue for the exotic gave rise to a huge demand for items such as carved ivory hunting horns from Africa. The 16th- and 17th-century Japanese Namban screens show the Portuguese trading in Japan. *Namban-jin* (barbarians from the south) is the name the Japanese gave to the Portuguese.

Silver, Gold and Jewellery

Among the ecclesiastical treasures are King Sancho I's 1214 gold cross and the 1506 Belém monstrance. The rich collection of jewels came from convents, originally donated by wealthy novices on entering religious orders.

Decorative Arts

Furniture, tapestries and textiles, liturgical vestments and bishops' mitres are among the wide range of objects on display. The furniture collection includes pieces from Portuguese and other European royal courts. Among the textiles are 17th-century bedspreads, tapestries (many of Flemish origin, such as the 16th-century Baptism of Christ), embroidered rugs and Arraiolos carpets.

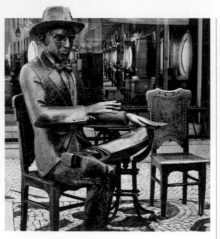

↑ Statue of poet Fernando Pessoa outside the café A Brasileira

EXPERIENCE MORE

Chiado

📍 M7 🚌 758 🚋 28
Ⓜ Baixa-Chiado

Statues of literary figures can be found in this area, known for its intellectual associations. A bronze statue by sculptor Lagoa Henriques depicts Fernando Pessoa, Portugal's great Modernist poet, sitting at a table outside the café A Brasileira, once a favourite rendezvous of the city's intellectuals.

Rua Garrett, named after the author and poet João Almeida Garrett (1799–1854), descending from Largo do Chiado towards the Baixa, is known for its cafés and shops. Devastated by fire in 1988, the former elegance of this quarter has now been restored.

Teatro Nacional de São Carlos

📍 M7 🏛 Rua Serpa Pinto 9 🚌 758, 790 🚋 28
Ⓜ Baixa-Chiado 🌐 tnsc.pt

Replacing a former opera house that was ruined by the earthquake of 1755, the Teatro de São Carlos was built in 1792–5 by José da Costa e Silva. Inspired by the design of great Italian theatres such as La Scala in Milan, the building has a beautifully proportioned façade and an enchanting Rococo interior. Views of the exterior, however, are spoiled by the car park, invariably crammed, which occupies the square in front.

The opera season lasts from September to June,

THE CHIADO FIRE

On 25 August 1988, a disastrous fire began in a store in Rua do Carmo, the street that links the Baixa with the Bairro Alto. Fire engines were unable to enter this pedestrianized street and the fire spread into Rua Garrett. Important 18th-century buildings were destroyed. The renovation project, headed by Portuguese architect Álvaro Siza Vieira, preserved many original façades.

but concerts and ballets are also staged here at other times of the year. The opera house is also home to the Portuguese Symphonic Orchestra.

São Roque

📍 M6 **🏠 Largo Trindade Coelho** **📞 213 235 444** **🚌 758** **🕐 Apr-Sep: 2-7pm Mon, 9am-7pm Tue-Sun (to 8pm Thu); Oct-Mar: 2-6pm Mon, 9am-6pm Tue-Sun** **🚫 Public hols**

São Roque's plain façade belies a rich interior. The church was founded at the end of the 16th century by the Jesuit Order, then at the peak of its power. In 1742, the Chapel of St John the Baptist was commissioned by the prodigal João V from Italian architects Luigi Vanvitelli and Nicola Salvi. Constructed in Rome and embellished with jewels, precious marbles, gold, silver and mosaics, the chapel was given the pope's blessing in the church of Sant'Antonio dei Portoghesi in Rome, dismantled and sent to Lisbon in three ships.

Among the church's many tiles, the oldest and most interesting are those in the third chapel on the right, dating from the 16th century and dedicated to São Roque (St Roch), protector against the plague. Other features of the church are the scenes of the Apocalypse painted on the ceiling.

Interior of São Roque, the earliest Jesuit church in Lisbon ↓

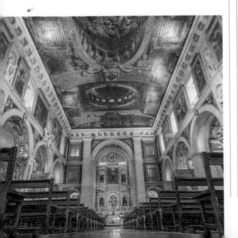

DRINK

Pavilhão Chinês
This quirky bar is packed with a bizarre array of collector's items, from dolls to model planes, and also features a strong cocktail list.

📍 L6 **🏠 Rua Dom Pedro V 89** **📞 213 424 729**

Cinco Lounge
Credited with making cocktails cool in Lisbon, this smart and very chic bar offers over 100 options, ranging from classics to the more experimental.

📍 L6 **🏠 Rua Ruben A. Leitão 17a** **🌐 cincolounge.com**

Portas Largas
A buzzy, traditional tavern with live music and well-priced drinks, where the revelry spills out onto the street.

📍 M6 **🏠 Rua da Atalaia 103-105** **📞 218 466 379**

Palácio de São Bento

Q K6 **A** Largo das Cortes **C** 213 919 620 **=** 790 **=** 28 **O** By appt last Sat of month, 3pm & 4pm **W** parlamento.pt

Also known as the Assembleia da República, this massive white Neo-Classical building started life in the late 1500s as the Benedictine monastery of São Bento. After the dissolution of the religious orders in 1834, the building became the seat of parliament, known as the Palácio das Cortes. The interior is grand with marble pillars and Neo-Classical statues.

Museu da Marioneta

Q K7 **A** Convento das Bernardas, Rua da Esperança 146 **=** 713, 727, 760 **=** 15, 25 **M** Cais do Sodré **A** Santos **O** 10am-6pm Tue-Sun **Q** 1 Jan, 1 May, 24 & 25 Dec **W** museudamarioneta.pt

This small puppet museum, housed in an elegantly refurbished convent building, includes characters from 17th- and 18th-century theatre and opera, including jesters, devils,

knights and satirical figures. Many of the puppets possess gruesome, contorted features that are unlikely to appeal to small children. The museum explains the history of the art form and runs videos of puppet shows. Check the website to see if a live performance is being held on the small stage. There is also a space for children's entertainment and learning.

Museu Nacional de Arte Contemporânea do Chiado

Q M7 **A** Rua Serpa Pinto 4-6 **=** 758, 790 **=** 28 **M** Baixa-Chiado **O** 10am-6pm Tue-Sun **Q** 1 Jan, Easter, 1 May, 25 Dec **W** museuarte contemporanea.gov.pt

The National Museum of Contemporary Art moved to this stylishly restored warehouse in 1994. The paintings and sculpture are arranged over three floors in seven rooms. Each room has a different theme illustrating the development from Romanticism to Modernism. The majority are Portuguese works, often showing a marked influence from other European countries – this is particularly noticeable in the 19th-century landscape painters who had contact with artists from the French Barbizon School.

The few international works of art on display are mainly French sculpture from the late 19th century, including one by Rodin (1840–1917). There are also temporary exhibitions, which are held for "very new artists, preferably inspired by the permanent collection".

→

Paintings and sculpture at Museu Nacional de Arte Contemporânea do Chiado

The delicate pillars and arcades of the Igreja do Carmo ↑

Igreja do Carmo

📍 M6 🏛 Largo do Carmo 📞 213 460 473
🚌 758 🚋 28 Ⓜ Baixa-Chiado 🕐 10am-6pm Mon-Sat (to 7pm Jun-Sep) 🔒 1 Jan, 1 May, 25 Dec

The Gothic ruins of this Carmelite church, built on a slope overlooking the Baixa, are evocative reminders of the devastation left by the earthquake of 1755. The church collapsed during Mass, depositing tons of masonry on to the people below. Founded in the late 14th century by Nuno Álvares Pereira, the commander who became a member of the Carmelite Order, the church was at one time the biggest in Lisbon. Today, the main body of the church and the chancel, whose roof withstood the earthquake, houses the Museu do Carmo, with a small, heterogeneous collection of sarcophagi, statuary, ceramics and mosaics. Among more ancient finds from Europe are a remnant of a Visigothic pillar and a Roman tomb carved with reliefs depicting the Muses. There are also finds from Mexico and South America, including ancient mummies.

EAT

A Brasileira

The intellectuals who made this 1905 café famous are gone, but its Art Deco interior and bar filled with tempting pastries remain a draw.

📍 M6 🏛 Rua Garrett 120 📞 213 469 541

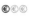

Páteo

Occupying a covered patio inside a former monastery, this lovely space specializes in quality fish and seafood, prepared by chef José Avillez.

📍 M6 🏛 Bairro do Avillez, 18 Rua Nova da Trindade 18 📞 215 830 290

Basílica da Estrela

Q J6 **A** Praça da Estrela **C** 213 960 915 **◰** 720, 738 **🚋** 25, 28 **🕒** 9am-1pm, 3-7:30pm Mon-Fri (to 8pm Sat & Sun); large groups by appointment

In the second half of the 18th century Maria I, daughter of José I, vowed she would build a church if she bore a son and heir to the throne. Her wish was granted and construction of the basilica began in 1779. Her son José, however, died of smallpox two years before the completion of the church in 1790.

The huge domed Basílica da Estrela, which is proudly set on a hill overlooking the west of the city, is one of Lisbon's most remarkable landmarks. A simpler version of the basilica at Mafra, this church was built by architects from the Mafra School in late-Baroque and Neo-Classical style. The façade is flanked by twin bell towers and decorated with an array of statues of saints and allegorical figures. The spacious, awe-inspiring interior, where light streams down from the pierced dome, is clad in grey, pink and yellow marble. The elaborate Empire-style tomb of Queen Maria I, who died in Brazil, lies in the right transept. Locked in a room nearby is Machado de Castro's extraordinary nativity scene, composed of over 500 cork-and-terracotta figures. To see and elms. The central feature of the park is a green wrought-iron bandstand, decorated with elegant filigree, where musicians strike up in the summer months. The bandstand was built in 1884 and originally stood on the Passeio Público, before the creation of Avenida da Liberdade.

The English Cemetery to the north of the gardens is best known as the burial place of Henry Fielding (1707–54), the English novelist and playwright who died in Lisbon at the age of 47. The *Journal of a Voyage to Lisbon*, published posthumously in 1775, recounts his last voyage to Portugal, made in a fruitless attempt to recover his failing health.

← The wrought-iron bandstand at the centre of Jardim da Estrela

it, ask the sacristan. Be sure to climb the dome's steep stone steps to access the flat roof above the Basilica, where you'll find breathtaking views of the western city – and down into the church below.

Jardim da Estrela

📍 K6 🏠 Praça da Estrela 🚌 720, 738 🚋 25, 28 Ⓜ Rato ⏰ 7am–midnight daily

Laid out in the middle of the 19th century, opposite the Basílica da Estrela, the popular gardens are a focal part of the Estrela quarter. Picturesque and serene, they provide an oasis from the hustle and bustle of the city. Local families congregate here at weekends to feed the carp and ducks in the lake, sit at the waterside café or wander among the flower beds, plants and trees. The formal gardens are planted with herbaceous borders and shrubs surrounding plane trees

 GREAT VIEW
Miradouro da São Pedro de Alcântara

This *miradouro* boasts a sweeping vista of eastern Lisbon. A tiled map, placed against the balustrade, helps you locate the landmarks. The view is most attractive at sunset and by night, when the castle is floodlit and the terrace becomes a meeting point for young Lisboetas.

Solar do Vinho do Porto

⦿ M6 **⌂** Rua de São Pedro de Alcântara 45 **☎** 213 475 707 **▭** 758 **⊞** 28 **⟳** Elevador da Glória: 11am–midnight Mon–Fri, 3pm–midnight Sat (times may vary, call ahead) **⟲** Public hols

The Portuguese word *solar* means mansion or manor house, and the Solar do Vinho do Porto occupies the ground floor of an 18th-century mansion. The building was once owned by the German architect Johann Friedrich Ludwig (Ludovice), who built the monastery at Mafra.

The port wine institute of Porto runs a pleasant bar here for the promotion of port. Nearly 200 types of port are listed in the lengthy drinks menu, with every producer represented and including some rarities. Unfortunately, many of the listed wines are often unavailable. All but the vintage ports are sold by the glass, with prices ranging from €1.50 for the simplest ruby to €13.30 for a glass of 40-year-old tawny.

Praça do Príncipe Real

⦿ L6 **▭** 758

Originally laid out in 1860 as a prime residential neighbourhood, Praça do Príncipe Real still retains its charming air of affluence. Smartly painted mansions surround a park with a café, statuary and some splendid robinia, magnolia and Judas trees. The branches of a huge cedar tree have been trained on a trellis, creating a wide shady spot for the locals who play cards beneath it. On the large square, at No 26, the eye-catching white

← The Time Out Market's cavernous food court, thronging with visitors

← The Time Out Market's cavernous food court, thronging with visitors

Neo-Moorish building with domes houses a shopping gallery.

Time Out Market (Mercado da Ribeira)

📍 M7 🏠 Avenida 24 de Julho 🕐 10am-midnight Sun-Wed, 10am-2am Thu-Sat; fish, fruit and vegetable market: 6am-2pm Mon-Sat 🌐 time outmarket.com

Lisbon's historic Mercado da Ribeira opened for business in 1930, and has served as the city's main fruit and vegetable market ever since. It was rejuvenated in 2014, by incorporating

the many food and drink stalls of the world's first Time Out Market, which now occupy most of the cavernous central hall. Stake your claim on one of the communal benches and sample the diverse array of produce on offer from some of Lisbon's best-known food outlets (including Henrique Sá Pessoa from Michelin-starred restaurant Alma). You can enjoy anything

from burgers and sushi to fine cheeses, *pastéis de nata* and ice cream, while champagne bars and wine, beer or juice stalls cater to the thirsty. There are further bars and restaurants around the outside of the market and on the first floor, which has a music venue for concerts. The concept has proved overwhelmingly successful – attracting over three million visitors a year and Time

CONTEMPORARY PORTUGUESE CUISINE

Exploding olives and acorn ice cream are some of the unusual offerings now found at Lisbon's innovative new restaurants. Spearheaded by the likes of José Avillez, creator of Belcanto, the first Lisbon restaurant to earn two Michelin stars, contemporary Portuguese dining focuses on finding unexpected, top-quality local ingredients to lift traditional recipes into something unforgettable.

← Tree-shaded park at the heart of Praça do Príncipe Real

A SHORT WALK
BAIRRO ALTO AND CHIADO

Distance 1 km (0.6 miles) **Nearest station** Baixa-Chiado metro **Time** 15 minutes

The Bairro Alto (high quarter) is a fascinating plot of cobbled streets adjacent to the Carmo and Chiado areas. Since the 1980s, this has been Lisbon's best-known nightlife zone, with countless small bars and restaurants alongside the older *casas de fado*. While more modern buildings have also sprung up in recent years, the quarter remains a lively, authentic part of the city to wander. In contrast, the Chiado presents a more manicured façade, filled as it is with elegant shops and old-style cafés that extend down from Praça Luís de Camões towards Rua do Carmo and the Baixa. Major renovation work has taken place here since a fire in 1988 destroyed many of the original buildings.

Praça Luís de Camões

RUA DO NORTE

RUA DAS GÁVEA

This statue of realist novelist Eça de Queirós (1845–1900), by Teixeira Lopes, was erected in 1903.

RUA DO ALECRIM

L. DO CHIADO

RUA GARRET

Tavares, at No 37 Rua da Misericórdia, first opened as a café in 1784 and is today an elegant restaurant with fine early-20th-century interiors.

Largo do Chiado, flanked by the churches of Loreto and Nossa Senhora da Encarnação.

Baixa-Chiado

A Brasileira, a historic café on Largo do Chiado adorned with gilded mirrors.

Rua Garrett, the Chiado's main shopping street.

0 metres	50
0 yards	50

N

The Museu de São Roque houses an interesting exhibition of religious artifacts and explains the history of the church next door.

FINISH

Opulent mosaics and semiprecious stones adorn the Baroque Capela de São João inside the 16th-century church of São Roque.

Cervejaria Trindade, a popular beer hall and restaurant decorated with azulejo panels.

Teatro da Trindade

Largo Rafael Bordalo Pinheiro, where the tiled façade of a house dating from 1864 features elaborate allegorical figures.

Igreja do Carmo, a Carmelite church whose graceful skeletal arches stand as a reminder of the earthquake of 1755. The chancel and main body of the church house an archaeological museum.

Elevador de Santa Justa, an ornate street lift offering direct access from the Baixa to the Bairro Alto district.

Shops in Rua do Carmo, restored and renewed after the devastating Chiado fire.

RUA DA MISERICÓRDIA
RUA NOVA DA TRINDADE
RUA DA TRINDADE
TRAVESSA DO CARMO
C. DO SACRAMENTO
LARGO DO CARMO

START

Locator Map

BAIRRO ALTO AND ESTRELA

↑ Diners seated along the patterned walls of the Cervejaria Trindade

BELÉM

Once the embarkation point for Portugal's intrepid seafaring explorers, this scenic waterfront suburb is perhaps best known for its dramatic Manueline monuments from that period. Belém also features more modern attractions – such as the Berardo Collection of contemporary art and the imposing Padrão dos Descobrimentos – which combine with the neighbourhood's spacious streets and well-maintained, leafy parks to make it a pleasant place to wander.

TORRE DE BELÉM

📍A10 🚶Avenida de Brasilia 🚌727, 728, 729, 751 🚋15 £Belém
🕐10am-6:30pm Tue-Sun (to 5:30pm Apr-Oct) 🚫1 Jan, Easter Sun,
1 May, 13 Jun, 25 Dec 🌐torrebelem.gov.pt

Set like a giant stone rook at the edge of the Tagus, this elaborate
tower showcases some of Belém's best Manueline architecture.
After admiring the intricate exterior, climb its narrow spiral
staircase for breathtaking views.

Commissioned by Manuel I, the tower was built as a fortress in 1514–20,
and soon became a symbol of Portugal's great era of expansion. The
real beauty of this Manueline gem lies in the decoration of the exterior.
Adorned with rope carved in stone, it has openwork balconies, Moorish-
style watchtowers and distinctive battlements in the shape of shields.
The Gothic interior below the terrace, which served as a storeroom
for arms and a prison, is very austere, but the private quarters in the
tower are worth visiting for the loggia and the panorama.

> 💬 **INSIDER TIP**
> **Aim High**
>
> Head to the former
> royal residences at
> the top of the tower
> to glimpse the most
> ornate carvings. Simple
> carvings adorn the old
> ammunitions store and
> prison rooms on the
> lower floors.

*Statue of the Virgin
Mary, a symbol of
protection for sailors.*

Sentry posts

*The vaulted dungeon
was used as a prison
until the 19th century.*

↑ The Torre de Belém, sitting at the edge of the Tagus river

Battlements, decorated with the cross of the Order of Christ.

The Italian-inspired arcaded loggia is a light touch along the battlements.

King's room

Entrance

↑ Open cloister in the tower, designed to dispel cannon smoke

Gangway to shore

Did You Know?

The tower's real name is the Torre de São Vicente, after the city's patron saint.

↑ The stone fortess, a symbol of Portgual's seafaring power

MOSTEIRO DOS JERÓNIMOS

📍 C9 🏛 Praça do Império (combined ticket for monastery and Torre de Belém available)
🚌 714, 727, 728, 729, 751 🚊 15 🚉 Belém 🕐 10am–5:30pm Tue–Sun (to 6:30pm May–Sep) 🚫 Public hols
🌐 mosteirojeronimos.gov.pt

Belém's most popular tourist attraction, this highly ornate monastery is a National Monument and was designated a UNESCO World Heritage Site in 1983.

A monument to the wealth of the Age of Discovery, the monastery was commissioned by Manuel I around 1501, and was financed largely by "pepper money" – a tax levied on spices, precious stones and gold. The monastery was cared for by the Order of St Jerome (Hieronymites) until 1834, when all religious orders were disbanded. Great figures from Portugal's history are entombed here – but one tomb stands empty: that of the "longed for" Dom Sebastião, the young king who never returned from battle in 1578.

The walls of the refectory are tiled with 18th-century azulejos.

Did You Know?

Eighteenth-century *azulejos* in the rectory depict the Feeding of the Five Thousand.

The modern wing, built in 1850 in Neo-Manueline style, houses the Museu Nacional de Arqueologia.

The west portal, designed by the French sculptor Nicolau Chanterène.

← The monastery's exterior, designed to emphasize the Portuguese empire's wealth

The chapterhouse holds the tomb of Alexandre Herculano, historian and first mayor of Belém.

Cloister

← The decorated exterior and interior of the Mosteiro dos Jerónimos

The chancel, commissioned in 1572 by Dona Catarina, the wife of João III.

The geometrical of the south portal are covered with exuberant decoration.

The empty tomb of the "longed for" Dom Sebastião.

EXPERIENCE MORE

Museu Nacional dos Coches

Q D9 **A** Avenida da Índia 136 **📷** 714, 727, 728, 729, 751 **🚋** 15 **Ⓡ** Belém **🕙** 10am-6pm Tue-Sun **🕙** 1 Jan, Easter, 1 May, 13 Jun, 24 & 25 Dec **W** museudoscoches.pt

This unique collection of coaches is arguably the finest in Europe. First established in the old Royal Riding School, the museum showcases a unique and opulent collection of coaches, carriages and sedan chairs dating from the 17th, 18th and 19th centuries. The collection was moved to a new, modern building by the Brazilian architect Paulo Mendes da Rocha, winner of the 2006 Pritzker Prize, in 2015.

The space enabled more modern vehicles to be added to the display. However, for most visitors the historic royal carriages still steal the show. Made in Portugal, Italy, France, Austria and Spain, carriages range from the plain to the preposterous. One of the earliest is the comparatively simple 17th-century leather and wood coach of Philip II of Spain. As time goes by, the coaches become more sumptuous, the interiors

lined with red velvet and gold, the exteriors carved and decorated with allegories and royal coats of arms. Three huge Baroque coaches made in Rome for the Portuguese ambassador to the Vatican, Dom Rodrigo Almeida e Menezes, Marquês de Abrantes, are the epitome of pomp, embellished with life-size gilded statues.

Further examples of royal carriages include two-wheeled cabriolets, landaus and pony-drawn chaises used by young members of the royal family. The 18th-century Eyeglass Chaise, whose black leather hood is pierced by sinister eye-like windows, was made during the Pombal era, when lavish decoration

was discouraged. The museology, installed in 2017, presents interactive displays that give context to the collection.

Jardim Botânico Tropical

Q C9 **A** Largo do Jerónimos **C** 213 921 851 **📷** 714, 727, 728, 729, 751 **🚋** 15 **Ⓡ** Belém **🕙** 9am-8pm daily (to 5pm Oct-Mar) **🕙** 1 Jan, Easter, 25 Dec

Also known as the Jardim do Ultramar, this peaceful park with ponds, waterfowl and peacocks attracts surprisingly few visitors. Designed at the beginning of the 20th century as the research centre of the Institute for Tropical Sciences, it is more of an arboretum than a flower garden. The emphasis is on rare and endangered tropical and subtropical trees and plants. Among the most striking are dragon trees, native to the Canary Islands and Madeira, monkey puzzle trees from South America and a splendid avenue of Washington palms. The charming Oriental garden with its streams, bridges and hibiscus is heralded by a large Chinese-style gateway that represented Macau in the Exhibition of the Portuguese World in 1940.

The research buildings are located in the neighbouring Palácio dos Condes da Calheta, whose interior walls are covered with *azulejos* that span three centuries. Temporary exhibitions are held in the palace (closed 12:30–2pm).

↑ An exhibition of pottery at the Museu Nacional de Arqueologia

Museu Nacional de Arqueologia

📍 B9 🏠 Praça do Império
🚌 714, 727, 728, 729, 751
🚋 15 🚉 Belém ⏰ 10am–6pm Tue–Sun ⏰ 1 Jan, Easter, 1 May, 13 Jun, 24 & 25 Dec 🌐 museunacional arqueologia.gov.pt

The long west wing of the Mosteiro dos Jerónimos, which was formerly the monks' dormitory, has been

←
Opulent carriages exibited at the Museu Nacional dos Coches

> **The long west wing of the Mosteiro dos Jerónimos, which was formerly the monks' dormitory, has been an archaeological museum since 1893.**

an archaeological museum since 1893. Reconstructed in the middle of the 19th century, the building is a poor imitation of the Manueline original. The museum houses Portugal's main archaeological research centre and the exhibits, from sites all over the country, include a gold Iron Age bracelet, Visigothic jewellery found in the Alentejo in southern Portugal, Roman ornaments, some fine Roman mosaics

and early-8th-century Moorish artifacts. The main Greco-Roman and Egyptian section is particularly strong on funerary art, featuring figurines, tombstones, masks, terracotta amulets and funeral cones inscribed with hieroglyphics alluding to the solar system, dating from 6000 BC.

The dimly lit Room of Treasures is full of exquisite gold and silver artifacts, including coins, necklaces, bracelets and other jewellery dating from 1800 to 500 BC. This room has been refurbished to allow more of the magnificent jewellery, unseen by the public for decades, to be displayed. In addition, the museum holds temporary exhibitions from time to time.

Museu de Marinha

📍 B9 🏛 Praça do Império
🚌 714, 727, 728, 729, 751
🚋 15 🚊 Belém 🕐 10am–
6pm daily (to 5pm Oct–
Apr) 📅 1 Jan, Easter,
1 May, 25 Dec ♿ ccm.
marinha.pt

The Maritime Museum was inaugurated in 1962 in the west wing of the Jerónimos monastery. It was here, in the chapel built by Henry the Navigator, that mariners took Mass before embarking on their voyages. A hall devoted to the Discoveries illustrates the progress in shipbuilding from the mid-15th century, capitalizing on the experience of long-distance explorers. Small replicas show the transition from the barque to the lateen-rigged caravel, through the faster square-rigged caravel, to the Portuguese *nau*.

Also here are navigational instruments, astrolabes and replicas of 16th-century maps showing the world as it was known then. The stone pillars, carved with the Cross of the Knights of Christ, are replicas of the types of *padrão* set up as monuments to Portuguese sovereignty on the lands discovered. A series of rooms displaying models of modern Portuguese ships leads on to the Royal Quarters, where

↑ Fine models of old sailing ships on display at the Museu de Marinha

you can see the exquisitely furnished wood-panelled cabin of King Carlos and Queen Amélia from the royal yacht *Amélia*, built in Scotland in 1900.

The modern, incongruous pavilion opposite houses original royal barges, the most extravagant of which is the royal brig built in 1780 for Maria I. The collection ends with an exhibition of seaplanes, including the *Santa Clara*, which made the first crossing of the South Atlantic, from Lisbon to Rio de Janeiro, in 1922.

Museu Colecção Berardo

📍 B9 🏛 Praça do Império
🚌 727, 728, 729, 751
🚋 15 🚊 Belém 🕐 10am–
7pm daily ♿ museu
berardo.pt

The brainchild of business mogul and art collector José Manuel Rodrigues Berardo, this fascinating gallery, in the Centro Cultural de Belém, boasts around 1,000 works by more than 500 artists. The Museu Colecção Berardo provides a rich compendium of a century of modern and contemporary art through a variety of media, from canvas to sculpture and from photography to video installations.

Highlights include Pablo Picasso's *Tête de Femme* (1909), a good example of the Spanish artist's Cubist style; variants of Andy Warhol's famous *Brillo Box* (1964–8); and Jeff Koons' *Poodle* (1991). Other artists on show include Francis Bacon, Willem de Kooning and Henry Moore. Notable Portuguese art on display includes Alberto Carneiro's sculptures and etchings by Paula Rego.

Centro Cultural de Belém

♀ B9 **⚐ Praça do Império** **🚌 714, 727, 728, 729, 751** **🚊 15** **🚋 Belém** **🕐 8am–8pm Mon–Fri, 10am–6pm Sat, Sun & public hols** **🌐 ccb.pt**

Standing between the Tagus and the Jerónimos monastery, this stark, modern building was erected as the headquarters of the Portuguese presidency of the European Community. In 1993 it opened as a cultural centre offering performing arts, music and photography. An exhibition centre houses the Museu Colecção Berardo.

Both the café and restaurant spill out onto the ramparts of the building, whose peaceful gardens look out over the quay and the river.

Padrão dos Descobrimentos

♀ C10 **⚐ Avenida de Brasília** **🚌 727, 728** **🚊 15** **🚋 Belém** **🕐 Mar–Sep: 10am–7pm daily; Oct–Feb: 10am–6pm Tue–Sun** **🚫 1 Jan, 1 May, 25 Dec** **🌐 padraodos descobrimentos.pt**

Standing prominently on the Belém water-front, this huge angular structure, the Padrão dos Descobrimentos (Monument to the Discoveries), was built in 1960 to mark the 500th anniversary of the death of Henry the Navigator. The 52-m- (170-ft-) high monument, commissioned by the Salazar regime, commemorates the mariners, royal patrons and all those who took part in the development of the Portuguese Age of Discovery. The monument is designed in the shape of a caravel, with Portugal's coat of arms on the sides and the sword of the Royal House of Avis rising above the entrance. Henry the Navigator stands at the prow with a caravel in hand. In two sloping lines either side of the monument are stone statues of Portuguese heroes linked with the Age of Discovery, such as Dom Manuel I holding an armillary sphere, the poet Camões with a copy of Os Lusíadas and the painter Nuno Gonçalves. On the monument's north side, the huge mariner's compass cut into the paving stone was a gift from South Africa in 1960. The central map, dotted with galleons and mermaids, shows the routes of the discoverers in the 15th and 16th centuries. Inside the monument, a lift (there is a fee) whisks you up to the sixth floor where steps then lead to the top for a splendid panorama of Belém. The basement level is used for temporary exhibitions.

The Padrão is not to everyone's taste but the setting is undeniably splendid and the caravel design is imaginative. The monument looks particularly dramatic when viewed from the west in the light of the late afternoon sun.

↓ Padrão dos Descobrimentos, inaugurated in 1960

Palácio de Belém

📍 C9 🏛 Praça Afonso de Albuquerque 🚌 714, 727, 728, 729, 751 🚊 15 🚉 Belém ⏰ 10:30am–4:30pm Sat; Museu da Presidência da República: 10am–6pm Tue–Sun 🔒 Easter, 1 May, 25 Dec 🌐 museu. presidencia.pt

Built by the Conde de Aveiras in 1559, before the Tagus had receded, this palace once had gardens bordering the river. In the 1700s it was bought by João V, who made it suitably lavish for his amorous liaisons. When the 1755 earthquake struck, the king, José I, and his family were staying here and thus survived the devastation of central Lisbon. Fearing another tremor, the royal family temporarily set up camp in tents in the palace grounds, while the interior was used as a hospital. Today the elegant pink building is the official residence of the President of Portugal.

The Museu da Presidência da República holds personal items and state gifts of former presidents, as well as the official portrait gallery.

Ermida de São Jerónimo

📍 A8 🏛 Praça de Itália 📞 210 966 989 🚌 714, 728, 729, 732, 751 ⏰ Mon–Sat (by appointment only)

Also known as the Capela de São Jerónimo, this little chapel was constructed in 1514 when Diogo Boitac was working on the Jerónimos monastery. Although a far simpler building, it is also

Manicured gardens of
the Palácio de Belém

Jerónimos monastery.
Inside, the planetarium
reveals the mysteries of
the cosmos. There are
shows in Portuguese,
English, Spanish and
French several times a
week, explaining the
movement of the stars
and our solar system, as
well as presentations
on the constellations or
the Star of Bethlehem
(Belém). The Hubble Vislon
show includes stunning
images provided by the
orbital telescope.

Manueline in style and
may have been built to a
design by Boitac. The only
decorative elements on
the monolithic chapel
are the four pinnacles,
corner gargoyles and
Manueline portal. Perched

Did You Know?

Monks used egg whites
to starch robes,
and gave the leftover
yolks to bakeries
to bake *pastéis
de Belém's*.

on a quiet hill above Belém,
the chapel has fine views. A
path from the terrace winds
down the hill towards the
Torre de Belém.

Planetário Calouste Gulbenkian

Q B9 **A** Praça do Império
🚌 714, 727, 728, 751
🚋 15 **Ⓜ** Belém **⏱** Times
vary, check website for
details **W** ccm.marinha.pt

Financed by the
Gulbenkian Foundation
and built in 1965, this
modern building sits
incongruously beside the

MAAT - Museu de Arte, Arquitetura e Tecnologia

Q D9 **🏛** Avenida Brasília
🚌 727, 728, 729 **🚊** 15
🚋 Belém **🕐** 11–7pm Wed-Mon **🔒** 1 Jan, 1 May & 25 Dec **🌐** maat.pt

With riverside views, the stylish Museu de Arte, Arquitetura e Tecnologia, popularly known as MAAT, is operated by the EDP Foundation, and is dedicated to contemporary art, primarily Portuguese, along with modern architecture and technology. Exhibits are housed in an award-winning building designed by the London-based architect Amanda Levete. Its structure is a sharp contrast to the well-known Lisbon power station, which stands next door and forms an integral part of this building complex. Visits to the MAAT include a tour of the iconic power station, and access to the building's undulating pedestrian roof which affords stunning views of Lisbon and the Tagus river.

As well as cutting-edge temporary exhibitions, the museum also features the Pedro Cabrita Reis Collection, which consists of some 400 works by over 70 artists from the end of the 20th century.

Igreja da Memória

Q C8 **🏛** Calçada do Galvão, Ajuda **☎** 213 635 295 **🚌** 728, 732
🚊 18 **🕐** For Mass: 6pm Mon-Sat, 10am Sun

Built in 1760, this church was founded by King José I in gratitude for his escape from an assassination plot on the site in 1758. The king was returning from a secret liaison with a lady of the noble Távora family when his carriage was attacked and a bullet hit him in the arm. Pombal used this as an excuse to get rid of his enemies in the Távora family, accusing them of conspiracy. In 1759 they were savagely tortured and executed. Their deaths are commemorated by a pillar in Beco do Chão Salgado, off Rua de Belém. The Neo-Classical domed church has a marble-clad interior and a small chapel, on the right, containing the tomb of Pombal, who died at the age of 83, a year after being banished from Lisbon.

Palácio Nacional da Ajuda

Q D7 **🏛** Largo da Ajuda
🚌 732, 742, 760 **🚊** 18
🕐 10am–5:30pm Thu-Tue (last adm 5pm) **🔒** 1 Jan, Easter, 1 May, 13 Jun, 25 Dec **🌐** palacioajuda.gov.pt

The royal palace, which was destroyed by fire in

→ MAAT, housed in an innovative building beside the Tagus river

1795, was replaced in the early 19th century by this magnificent Neo-Classical building set around a large quadrangle. It was left incomplete when the royal family was forced into exile in Brazil in 1807, following the invasion of Portugal.

The palace only became a permanent residence of the royal family when Luís I became king in 1861 and married an Italian Princess, Maria Pia di Savoia. No expense was spared in furnishing the apartments, which are decorated with silk wallpaper, Sèvres porcelain and crystal chandeliers. A prime example of regal excess is the extraordinary Saxe Room, a wedding present to Maria Pia from the King of Saxony, in which every piece of furniture is decorated

↑ Manicured formal gardens of the Jardim Botânico da Ajuda

with Meissen porcelain. On the first floor, the huge Banqueting Hall, with crystal chandeliers, silk-covered chairs and an allegory of the birth of João VI on the frescoed ceiling, is truly impressive. At the other end of the palace, Luís I's Neo-Gothic painting studio is a more intimate display of intricately carved furniture.

Jardim Botânico da Ajuda

📍 C7 🏠 Calçada da Ajuda 🚌 714, 727, 728, 729, 732 🚊 18 🕐 9am–6pm daily (to 8pm May-Sep) 📅 1 Jan, 25 Dec 🌐 isa.ulisboa.pt/jba

Laid out on two levels by Pombal in 1768,

these Italian-style gardens provide a pleasant respite from the noisy suburbs of Belém. The entrance on Calçada da Ajuda (wrought-iron gates in a pink wall) is easy to miss.

The park comprises 5,000 plant species from Africa, Asia and America. Notable features are the 400-year-old dragon tree, native of Madeira, and the flamboyant 18th-century fountain decorated with serpents, winged fish, sea horses and mythical creatures. A majestic terrace looks out over the lower level of the gardens.

A SHORT WALK
BELÉM

Distance 1.5 km (1 mile) **Nearest station** Mosteiro dos Jerónimos tram stop **Time** 25 minutes

Portugal's former maritime glory, expressed in imposing, exuberant buildings such as the Jerónimos monastery, is evident everywhere in Belém. Silted up since the days of the caravels, this picturesque area along the waterfront was restructured at Salazar's insistence, in an attempt to revive awareness of and celebrate the country's Golden Age. A stroll here is consequently littered with historically significant sights: Praça do Império was laid out for the 1940 Exhibition of the Portuguese World, while Praça Afonso de Albuquerque was dedicated to Portugal's first viceroy of India. The Palácio de Belém, restored in the 18th century, briefly housed the royal family after the earthquake of 1755.

Mosteiro dos Jerónimos, a former monastery covered in rich Manueline decoration.

LARGO DOS JERÓNIMOS

PRAÇA DO IMPÉRIO

The Museu Nacional de Arqueologia exhibits archaeological finds ranging from an Iron Age gold bracelet to Moorish artifacts.

Praça do Império, a great square in front of the monastery, whose central fountain is lit up on special occasions.

START

| 0 metres | 50 |
| 0 yards | 50 |

N ↑

Jardim Botânico Tropical, peaceful gardens filled with exotic plants and trees gathered from Portugal's former colonies.

Locator Map

Palácio de Belém, a former royal palace that is now the residence of the Portuguese president.

TRAVESSA DOS FERREIROS

RUA DE BELÉM

FINISH

RUA VIEIRA PORTUENSE

Stop at *Antiga Confeitaria de Belém*, the birthplace of *pastéis de Belém (rich custard tarts)*.

Rua Vieira Portuense is lined with colourful 16th- and 17th-century houses and runs alongside a small park.

Praça Afonso de Albuquerque, a public square with a central Neo-Manueline statue of the first Portuguese viceroy of India, after whom the space is named.

The Cristo Rei sculpture glimpsed through the red towers of the Ponte 25 de Abril

BEYOND THE CENTRE

Outside the city centre, there are still an impressive number of sights to be found. Parque Eduardo VII, with its sharply edged hedges and expansive *miradouro*, is a welcome green space for visitors to Lisbon, while the astounding collections of the nearby Museu Calouste Gulbenkian make for a rewarding visit. The brick-red Ponte 25 de Abril also stands in this area, stretching dramatically to the opposite bank of the Tagus, where the Christo Rei monument towers above the city.

MUSEU CALOUSTE GULBENKIAN

🏠 Avenida de Berna 45A 🚌 713, 716, 726, 742, 746, 756
Ⓜ Praça de Espanha or São Sebastião 🕐 10am-6pm
Wed-Mon (free Sun after 2pm) 🚫 1 Jan, Easter, 1 May,
24 & 25 Dec 🌐 gulbenkian.pt/museu

6,000

The approximate
number of artworks
Gulbenkian amassed
in his personal
collection.

Thanks to wealthy Armenian oil magnate Calouste
Gulbenkian's wide-ranging tastes and his eye for a
masterpiece, this museum has one of the finest
collections of art in Europe.

The museum's works are split across two
separately housed collections, linked by a
serene stretch of urban park. The Founder's
Collection – Gulbenkian's personal pieces –
sits within a purpose-built museum dating
from 1969, with varied exhibits ranging from
ancient Egyptian statuettes to an astonishing
array of René Lalique Art Nouveau jewellery.
South of the gardens stands the Modern
Collection, widely considered to be the world's
most complete collection of modern Portuguese art. Standard tickets allow access to
both collections, while the sculpture-dotted
gardens can be explored free of charge.

CALOUSTE GULBENKIAN

Born in Scutari in 1869, Gulbenkian
started his art collection at the age of
14, when he bought some ancient coins
in a bazaar. In 1928, he was granted a 5
per cent stake in four major oil companies, earning himself the nickname
"Mr Five Per Cent". With the wealth he
accumulated, Gulbenkian was able to
indulge his love of fine art. During World
War II, he went to live in neutral Portugal,
and bequeathed his estate to his adopted
nation upon his death in 1955.

Exhibits within the ↑
museum's extensive
Modern Collection

The blocky concrete building in which the Founder's Collection is housed

This fine marble statue of Diana, goddess of the hunt, is part of the Founder's Collection

FOUNDER'S COLLECTION

Ranking alongside the Museu de Arte Antiga as the finest museum in Lisbon, the Founder's Collection exhibits, which span over 4,000 years from ancient Egyptian figurines, through translucent Islamic glassware, to Art Nouveau brooches, are displayed in spacious and well-lit galleries, many overlooking the gardens or courtyards. Although the museum is not large, each work of art is worthy of attention.

In the Egyptian, Classical and Mesopotamian gallery priceless treasures chart the evolution of Egyptian art from the Old Kingdom (c 2700 BC) to the Roman Period (from the 1st century BC). Outstanding pieces in the Classical art section include a

magnificent red figure Greek vase, and a Roman satyr's head from the 2nd century AD.

The museum's Eastern art is also remarkable. Being Armenian, Gulbenkian had a keen interest in works from the Near and Middle East, resulting in a fine collection of Persian and Turkish carpets, textiles, costumes and ceramics in the Oriental Islamic gallery. In terms of Far Eastern pieces, there is a large collection of Chinese porcelain acquired by Gulbenkian between 1907 and 1947. One of the

rarest pieces is a small blue-glazed bowl from the Yuan Dynasty (1271–1368).

The carefully plotted route around the museum ends with a room filled with the flamboyant Art Nouveau creations of French jeweller René Lalique (1860–1945). Gulbenkian was a close friend of Lalique's and acquired many of the pieces on display directly from the artist. Inlaid with semiprecious stones and covered with enamel or gold leaf, the ornate collection constitutes a spectacular finish to this unique and incredibly diverse museum.

→

Porcelain vases on display within the Founder's Collection

Visitor wandering the galleries of the Founder's Collection ↑

Busts on display in the Modern Collection ↑

Must See

Busts on display in the Modern Collection ↑

TOP 5 FOUNDER'S COLLECTION PIECES

St Catherine
A serene 15th-century bust, painted by the Flemish artist Rogier van der Weyden.

Boy Blowing Bubbles
Édouard Manet's 1867 painting considers the transience of life and art.

Yuan Dynasty Stem Cup
This blue-glazed piece is decorated with delicate reliefs of Taoist figures under bamboo leaves.

Diana Statue
A graceful marble statue, once owned by Catherine the Great and considered too obscene to exhibit.

Ancient Greek Vase
This 5th century BC vase is adorned with mythological motifs.

Did You Know?

Paula Rego's pieces have fetched up to £1.1 million at auction, a record for a Portuguese artist.

MODERN COLLECTION

The Modern Collection lies across the gardens from the Founder's Collection and is part of the same cultural foundation. It is housed in a large, light-filled building, designed by architect Sir Leslie Martin in 1983.

The permanent collection features over 10,000 works, with an emphasis on paintings and sculpture by Portuguese artists from the turn of the 20th century to the present day. Perhaps the most famous painting is the striking portrait of poet Fernando Pessoa in the Café Irmãos Unidos (1964) by José de Almada Negreiros (1893–1970), a leading exponent of Portuguese Modernism. The oil painting was commissioned by the Calouste Gulbenkian Foundation, and intended to replicate a similar portrait that Almada had produced for the café itself.

Also of interest are paintings by Eduardo Viana

(1881–1967), Amadeo de Sousa Cardoso (1887–1910) and contemporary artists such as Rui Sanches, Graça Morais, Teresa Magalhães and – perhaps the best known – Paula Rego. Rego settled in London in the mid-1970s, but she has long been hailed in Portugal as one of the nation's greatest living artists. Her work often contains elements of magical realism, although later works have gradually tended towards more realistic renderings.

Within the international collection are works by big hitters such as David Hockney and British sculptor Antony Gormley (renowned for his *Angel of the North* sculpture in Gateshead, England).

As well as the exhibition space, which comprises three linked galleries, there is also an events area, a busy café and a museum bookshop.

MUSEU NACIONAL DO AZULEJO

🏠 Rua da Madre de Deus 4 🚌 718, 728, 742, 759, 794 🕐 10am–6pm Tue–Sun 🚫 Mon, public hols 🌐 museudoazulejo.gov.pt

Housed in a beautiful 16th-century convent, the National Tile Museum offers an unmatched display of this uniquely Portuguese art form, with *azulejos* dating from the 15th century right through to the present day.

Dona Leonor, widow of King João II, founded the Convento da Madre de Deus in 1509. Built in Manueline style, restorations of the church under João III and João V added its simple Renaissance designs and striking Baroque decoration. The stunning convent cloisters are now home to the National Tile Museum. Decorative panels and individual tiles trace the evolution of tile-making from its Moorish roots up to the current Portuguese art form. The walls of the restaurant are lined with 19th-century tiles, depicting hanging game, from wild boar and pheasants to fish.

📷 **PICTURE PERFECT**
Manueline Designs

Set around a central courtyard, the cloister is a serene spot. Its delicate columns and carved vaulted walkways are the perfect place to point your lens.

Fine 17th-century tiles patterning the cloister ↑ from the original convent

The 16th-century church of Madre de Deus acquired its sumptuous interiors under João V. The Rococo altarpiece was added after the earthquake of 1755

↑ Fine 17th-century tiles patterning the cloister from the original convent

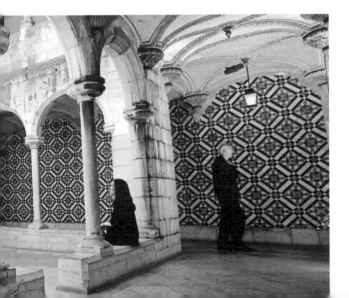

EXPERIENCE MORE

Praça Marquês de Pombal

🚌 711, 712, 720 & many other routes
Ⓜ Marquês de Pombal

At the top of Avenida da Liberdade, traffic thunders round the "Rotunda" (roundabout), as the *praça* is also known. At the centre is a lofty 1934 monument to Pombal. The despotic states-man, who virtually ruled Portugal from 1750 to 1777, stands on the top of the column, his hand on a lion (a symbol of power) and his eyes directed down to the Baixa, whose creation he masterminded. Allegorical images depicting Pombal's political, educational and agricultural reforms decorate the base of the monument. Although greatly feared, this dynamic politician propelled the country into the Age of Enlightenment. Broken blocks of stone at the foot of the monument and tidal waves flooding the city are an allegory of the destruction caused by the 1755 earthquake.

Nearby, the well-tended Parque Eduardo VII extends northwards behind the square. The paving stones around the Rotunda are decorated with a mosaic of Lisbon's coat of arms. Many of the city's sightseeing operators have their main pick-up located at the bottom of Parque Eduardo VII. There is also a multilingual booth where visitors can buy tickets and plan excursions.

Cristo Rei

🏛 Santuário Nacional do Cristo Rei, Alto do Pragal, Almada 🚢 from Cais do Sodré to Cacilhas then 🚌 101 🕐 9:30am–6pm daily (to 6:45pm Jul–Sep) 🌐 cristorei.pt

Modelled on the Cristo Redentor in Rio de Janeiro (Brazil), this giant-sized statue stands with arms outstretched on the south bank of the Tagus river. The impressive 28-m-(92-ft-) tall figure of Christ, mounted on an 82-m (269-ft) pedestal, was sculpted by Francisco Franco in 1949–59 at the instigation of Prime Minister Salazar.

You can see the monument from various viewpoints in the city, but it is fun to take a ferry from Cais do Sodré to the Margem Sul (the south bank, which until recently was simply known as the Outra Banda, or "other bank"), then a bus or taxi to the monument. A lift plus some steps take you 82 m (269 ft) up to the top of the pedestal, afford-ing fine views of the city and river below.

Parque Eduardo VII

🏠 Praça Marquês de Pombal ☎ 213882 278 🚌 711, 712, 720 Ⓜ Marquês de Pombal 🕐 Estufa Fria: 10am–7pm daily (Nov–Mar: 9am–5pm) 🚫 1 Jan, 1 May, 25 Dec

Central Lisbon's largest park was named after King Edward VII of the United Kingdom, who came to Lisbon in 1902 to reaffirm the Anglo-Portuguese alliance.

The wide grassy slope, which extends for 25 hectares (62 acres), was laid out as Parque da Liberdade, a continuation of Avenida da Liberdade, in the late 19th century. Neatly clipped box hedging, flanked by mosaic patterned walkways, stretches uphill from the Praça Marquês de Pombal to a belvedere at the top. Here you will find a flower-filled garden dedicated to the memory of renowned Portuguese *fado* singer Amália Rodrigues, and a pleasant café. The vantage point at the summit of the park offers fine, sweeping views of the city. On clear days you can see as far as the Serra da Arrábida,

← The mammoth Cristo Rei statue, soaring high into the sky

↑ Expansive views of the city from the *miradouro* of Parque Eduardo VII

a nature reserve located 40km (25 miles) from the city centre.

Situated in the northwest corner, the most inspiring feature of this park is the jungle-like Estufa Fria, or greenhouse, where exotic plants, streams and waterfalls provide serene respite from the city streets. At this urban oasis there are in fact three greenhouses: in the Estufa Fria (cold greenhouse), palms push through the slatted bamboo roof and paths wind through a forest of ferns, fuchsias, flowering shrubs and banana trees; the warmer Estufa Quente and Estufa Doce are filled with tropical plants, water-lily ponds and impressive cacti. Near

> 💬 INSIDER TIP
> **River Views**
>
> Take the passenger ferry from Cais do Sodré across the Tagus to the little port of Cacilhas, where you'll find many riverfront seafood restaurants and great views of Lisbon back across the water.

the *estufas*, a pond with carp and a galleon-shaped play area are popular with children.

On the east side, the Pavilhão Carlos Lopes, named after the 1984 Olympic marathon winner, was extensively refurbished in 2016 and is now used for concerts, exhibitions and conferences.

Ponte 25 de Abril

🚌 753

Once called the Ponte Salazar after the dictator who had it built in 1966, Lisbon's suspension bridge was renamed to commemorate the revolution of 25 April 1974 that restored democracy to Portugal.

Inspired by San Francisco's Golden Gate Bridge in the US, this steel construction stretches for 2 km (1 mile). The lower tier was modified in 1999 to accommodate the Fertagus, a railway across the Tagus. The bridge's notorious traffic congestion has been partly resolved by the opening of the 17-km (11-mile) Vasco da Gama bridge. Spanning the Tagus river from Montijo to Sacavém, north of the Parque das Nações, this bridge was completed in 1998.

↑ Ponte 25 de Abril illuminated at night, with the city lights behind

Fundação Oriente Museu

🏛 Avenida Brasília, Doca de Alcântara Norte 🚌 712, 714, 728, 738, 742 ⏰ 10am–6pm Tue–Sun (to 10pm Fri) 🌐 museudooriente.pt

This museum and cultural centre is dedicated to showing the historical and cultural links between Portugal and its former colonies in the East. The permanent exhibition is split into two collections. The Portuguese Presence in Asia has a selection of exhibits ranging from furniture and jewellery to porcelain, paintings and textiles.

Highlights include 17th- and 18th-century Chinese and Japanese folding screens and some rare examples of Namban art – Portuguese-influenced Japanese art of the 16th and 17th centuries.

The second exhibition is the Kwok On Collection, which features the performing arts of a vast geographic area extending from Turkey to Japan. It includes fine masks from Asia and a section on shadow and puppet theatre from India, China and Indonesia.

Doca de Santo Amaro

🚌 714, 727, 732, 751, 756 🚊 15 🚇 Alcântara-Mar

In the early 1930s, Lisbon's docks at Alcântara were the city's main access point. As the importance of the docks declined, the once-industrial riverside has been opened up. One of the best places to head for is the Doca de Santo Amaro, a largely enclosed dock that sits below the humming traffic of the dramatic Ponte 25 de Abril. The inner edge of the docks is lined with former warehouses, converted in the 1990s and now housing cafés, restaurants and bars with fine views over the water. These tend to be popular, and tables on the outside terraces get snapped up quickly.

Beneath the bridge to the west of the docks is a strange, boomerang-shaped structure, designed to stop falling debris. Continue past this and it's a good 20-minute walk to Belém.

Museu da Carris
🏠 Rua 1 de Maiao
🚍 714, 727, 732
🕐 10am-6pm Tue-Sat
🌐 museu.carris.pt

Carris is the company that runs Lisbon's surface public transport and this museum details the history of a system that has had to negotiate a broad river estuary

and some serious hills since 1872. Set in a sprawling former tram depot, the museum is divided into three zones. The first uses various exhibits to trace the development of Lisbon's public transport. You can then take a fun trip on a tram to the other two zones, which are filled with historic trams and buses, including early horse-drawn varieties.

Down by the river at the bottom of the site, a collection of old shipping containers and double-decker buses make up Village Underground, an innovative work space for Lisbon's creative set.

LX Factory
🏠 Rua Rodrigues Faria 103 🚍 201, 742, 751, 756, 760 🌐 lxfactory.com

Virtually beneath the Ponte 25 de Abril in a slightly

GREAT VIEW
**Ponte 25
de Abril**

For a unique experience take the lift up Pillar 7 of this landmark bridge, which offers unbroken views across the river and the city's south bank from 80 m (262 ft) above the waves. Tickets cost around €6.

shabby part of town, LX Factory is one of the hippest places in Lisbon. The complex is inside a huge former textiles plant, with the warehouses, factory spaces and courtyards transformed into studios and workshops for the arts, fashion and creative media. Woven among them are innovative restaurants, bars, cafés and shops. Visit on Sunday morning when a lively flea market takes place.

Shelves stacked to the ceiling at Ler Devagar bookshop in LX Factory

Museu da Água

🏠 Rua do Alviela 12
📞 218 100 215 🚌 735
🕐 10am–5:30pm daily
🚫 Public hols

Dedicated to the history of Lisbon's water supply, this informative museum was imaginatively created around the city's first steam pumping station. It commemorates Manuel da Maia, the 18th-century engineer behind the Águas Livres aqueduct.

Pride of place goes to four lovingly preserved steam engines, one of which still functions (by electricity). The development of technology relating to the city's water supply is documented with photographs. Particularly interesting is the exhibit on the Alfama's 17th-century Chafariz d'El Rei, one of Lisbon's first fountains. Locals used to queue at one of six founts, depending on their social status.

Campo Pequeno

🚌 736, 744 Ⓜ Campo Pequeno
🕐 Bullring: 10am–11pm daily

This square is dominated by the red-brick Neo-Moorish bullring built in the late 19th century. The building has undergone development, and a car park and leisure centre have been added. Much of the bullring's distinctive architecture, such as keyhole-shaped windows and double cupolas, have been retained.

Museu de Lisboa

🏠 Campo Grande 245
🚌 736, 747, 750 Ⓜ Campo Grande 🕐 10am–6pm Tue–Sun 🚫 1 Jan, 1 May, 25 Dec 🌐 museude lisboa.pt

Palácio Pimenta was allegedly commissioned by João V for his mistress Madre Paula, a nun from the nearby convent at Odivelas. When the mansion was built, in the middle of the 18th century, it occupied a peaceful site outside the city. Nowadays it has to contend with the traffic of Campo Grande. The house itself, however, retains its period charm. The displays follow the development of the city, from prehistoric times through the Romans,

Visigoths and Moors, traced by means of drawings tiles, paintings, models and historical documents. Notable exhibits are those depicting the city before the earthquake of 1755, including a highly detailed model made in the 1950s and an impressive 17th-century oil painting by Dirk Stoop (1610–86) of *Terreiro do Paço*, as Praça do Comércio was known then. One room is devoted to the Águas Livres aqueduct, with architectural plans as well as prints and watercolours of the completed aqueduct.

The earthquake theme is resumed with pictures of the city amid the devastation and various plans for its reconstruction. The museum brings you into the 20th century with a large colour poster celebrating the Revolution of 1910 and the proclamation of the new republic.

Oceanário de Lisboa

⌂ Esplanada Dom Carlos 1, Parque das Nações ▦ 705, 725, 728, 744, 750, 782 Ⓜ Oriente ⓡ Oriente ⓒ 10am-8pm daily (to 7pm Nov-Mar) Ⓦ oceanario.pt

The main attraction at Parque das Nações, the oceanarium was designed by American architect Peter Chermayeff, and is perched on the end of a pier. It holds an impressive array of species – birds and some mammals as well as fish and other underwater dwellers. Landscapes represent the habitats of the Atlantic, Pacific, Indian and Antarctic oceans, with suitable fauna and flora. The aquarium's vast central tank has a dazzling variety of fish, large and

← Neo-Moorish façade of the bullring in Campo Pequeno

↑ Visitors watching the fish in the central tank at Oceanário de Lisboa

small. Sharks co-exist peaceably with bream in the softly lit waters.

Parque das Nações

⌂ Avenida Dom João II ▦ 705, 725, 728, 744, 750, 782 Ⓜ Oriente ⓡ Oriente ⓒ Park: 24 hours daily; Pavilhão do Conhecimento: 10am-6pm Tue-Fri, 11am-7pm Sat & Sun ⓒ 1 Jan, 24, 25 & 31 Dec Ⓦ portaldas nacoes.pt

Originally the site of Expo 98, Parque das Nações is now a Lisbon hub. With its contemporary architecture and family-oriented attractions, the park has renewed the eastern waterfront, which was once an industrial

wasteland. The soaring geometry of the platform canopies over Santiago Calatrava's Oriente Station set the architectural tone. The Portugal Pavilion has a large reinforced concrete roof suspended like a sailcloth above its forecourt.

Pavilhão do Conhecimento – Ciencia Viva is a fascinating modern museum of science and technology that houses several interactive exhibitions.

Spectacular views can be had from the cable car that links the Torre Vasco da Gama with the marina. The promenade along the river also offers delightful views, including of the Vasco da Gama bridge. Also in the area is the MEO Arena.

Aqueduto das Águas Livres

📍 Best seen from Calçada da Quintinha 🚍 774, 783 🕐 10am-5:30pm Tue-Sun; Mãe d'Água das Amoreiras: 10am-12:30pm, 1:30-5:30 Tue-Sun 🔒 Public hols

Considered the most beautiful sight in Lisbon at the turn of the 20th century, the impressive structure of Aqueduto das Águas Livres looms over the Alcântara valley northwest of the city. The construction of an aqueduct gave João V the opportunity to indulge his passion for grandiose building schemes, as the only area of Lisbon with fresh drinking water was the Alfama. A tax on meat, wine, olive oil and other comestibles funded the project, and although not complete until the 19th century, it was already supplying the city with water by 1748. The main pipeline measures 19 km

(12 miles), but the total length, including all the secondary channels, is 58 km (36 miles). The most visible part of this imposing structure are the 35 arches crossing the Alcântara valley, the tallest of which rise to 65 m (213 ft) above ground.

It is possible to take guided tours over the Alcântara arches. There are also tours of the Mãe d'Água reservoir and trips to the Mãe d'Água springs. Contact the Museu da Água for details of the trips.

At the end of the aqueduct, the Mãe d'Água das Amoreiras is a castle-like building that served as a reservoir for the water supplied from the aqueduct. Today the space is used for art exhibitions, fashion shows and other events.

Parque do Monteiro-Mor

📍 Largo Júlio Castilho 📞 217 567 620 🚍 703, 736, 796 Ⓜ Lumiar 🕐 Park: 2-6pm Tue, 10am-10pm Wed-Sun

Monteiro-Mor park was sold to the state in 1975 and the 18th-century palace buildings were converted to museums. The gardens are attractive; much of the land is wooded, though the area around the museums has gardens with flowering shrubs, duck ponds and tropical trees.

The slightly old-fashioned Museu Nacional do Traje (Costume Museum) has a vast collection of textiles, accessories and costumes worn by people of note. The

Did You Know?

Aqueduto das Águas Livres only stopped supplying water for human consumption in the 1960s.

Tiled terrace, decorated with figures leading to the chapel of the Palácio Fronteira

Museu Nacional do Teatro has two buildings: one devoted to temporary exhibitions, the other containing a small permanent collection. Photographs, posters and cartoons feature famous 20th-century Portuguese actors, and one section is devoted to Amália Rodrigues, the famous *fado* singer.

Palácio Fronteira

🏠 Largo São Domingos de Benfica 1 📞 217 782 023 🚌 770 Ⓜ Jardim Zoológico 🚇 Benfica 🕐 By tour only Jun–Sep: 10:30, 11am, 11:30am, noon; Oct–May: 11am, noon 🚫 Sun, public hols

This country manor house was built as a hunting pavilion for João de

Imposing arches of the Aqueduto das Águas Livres

Mascarenhas, the first Marquês de Fronteira, in 1640. Although skyscrapers are visible in the distance, it still occupies a quiet spot, by the Parque Florestal de Monsanto. Both house and garden have *azulejo* decoration whose subjects include battle scenes and trumpet-blowing monkeys.

Although the palace is still occupied by the 12th marquis, some living rooms and the library, as well as the formal gardens, are included in the tour. The Battles Room has lively tiled panels depicting scenes of the War of Restoration (1640–68), with a detail of João de Fronteira fighting a Spanish general. It was his loyalty to Pedro II during this war that earned him the title of Marquês. Interesting comparisons can be made between these 17th-century Portuguese tiles and the Delft ones in the dining room, depicting naturalistic scenes. The dining room is decorated

with frescoed panels and portraits of Portuguese nobility. The late-16th-century chapel is the oldest part of the house. The façade is adorned with stones, shells, broken glass and bits of china. These fragments of crockery are believed to have been used at the feast inaugurating the palace and then smashed to ensure no one else could sup off the same set. Visits to the garden start at the chapel terrace, where tiled niches are decorated with figures personifying the arts and mythological creatures.

In the formal Italian garden the immaculate box hedges are cut into shapes to represent the seasons of the year. To one end, tiled scenes of dashing knights on horseback, representing ancestors of the Fronteira family, are reflected in the waters of a large tank. On either side of the water, a grand staircase leads to a terrace above. Here, decorative niches contain the busts of Portuguese kings and colourful majolica reliefs adorn the arcades. More blue-and-white tiled scenes, realistic and allegorical, decorate the wall at the far end of the garden.

THE LISBON COAST

With so much on offer in the city itself, it can be easy to forget that pristine beaches and shady woodland lie just a short distance away. Head northwest to the palace-dotted hills of Sintra, a must-do trip that can be squeezed into a day – although in this atmospheric town packed with spectacular architecture and exotic gardens, there's plenty to keep you there longer. Also within reach are the golden sands of Caparica and the Tróia Peninsula, while south of the Tagus sits the Serra da Arrábida, a wild, wooded mountain range that's ripe for exploring.

Sintra's spectacular skyline, dominated by the Palácio Nacional ↑

SINTRA

29 km (18 miles) NW of Lisbon 🚇 🚌 Avenida Dr Miguel Bombarda; bus 434 runs from station to all the major sights 🛈 Praça da República 23; 219 231 157

Sintra's stunning setting on the north slopes of the granite Serra made it a favourite summer retreat for the kings of Portugal – resulting in the construction of a number of quirkily spectacular palaces. Today, the town (recognized as a UNESCO Cultural Landscape Site in 1995) draws thousands of visitors all through the year. Nevertheless, many quiet walks can be found in the beautiful surrounding wooded hills.

Museu de História Natural de Sintra

🏠 Rua do Paço 20
📞 219 238 563
🕐 10am–6pm
Tue–Fri, 12–6pm Sat & Sun 🚫 Mon and public hols

Located in the town's historic centre, Sintra's excellent natural history museum features a huge permanent collection of fossils and other ancient exhibits dating back several millennia. Housed in a striking 19th-century building, the museum also hosts regular temporary exhibitions relating to Portugal's natural history.

Museu das Artes de Sintra

🏠 Avenida Helliodoro Salgado 📞 965 233 692
🕐 Apr–Sep: 10am–8pm Tue–Fri, 2–8pm Sat & Sun; Oct–Mar: 10am–6pm Tue–Fri, 12–6pm Sat & Sun 🚫 Public hols

This museum displays Portuguese and international artworks,

with the permanent exhibition featuring the private collections of Emílio Paula Campos and Dórita Castel-Branco, and several landscapes of Sintra dating from the mid-18th century.

Parque da Pena

🏠 Estra da Pena 🕐 Mar-late Oct: 9:30am-8pm daily; Nov-early Mar: 10am-6pm daily (last adm 1 hour before closing) 🚫 1 Jan, 25 Dec 🌐 parquesdesintra.pt

A huge park surrounds the Palácio Nacional da Pena, and hidden among the foliage are gazebos, follies and fountains, and a chalet built by Fernando II for his second wife, the Countess of Edla, in 1869. Cruz Alta, the highest point of the Serra at 529 m (1,740 ft), commands spectacular views of the Serra and surrounding plain. On a nearby crag is a statue known as "The Warrior", which supposedly symbolizes the king watching over his park and palace.

Castelo dos Mouros

🏠 Estrada da Pena 🕐 Mar-late Oct: 9:30am-8pm daily; Nov-early Mar: 10am-6pm daily (last adm 1 hour before closing) 🚫 1 Jan, 25 Dec 🌐 parquesdesintra.pt

Above the old town, the ramparts of the 10th-century Moorish castle conquered by Afonso Henriques in 1147 snake over the top of the Serra. On a fine day, there are great views from the castle walls over the old town to Palácio Nacional da Pena and along the coast. Hidden inside the walls is an ancient Moorish cistern, while the gateway's carved monogram ("DFII") is a reminder that Fernando II restored the castle in the 19th century.

Quinta da Regaleira

🏠 Rua Barbosa du Bocage 🚌 435 🕐 9:30am-6pm daily (to 8pm Apr-Sep) 🌐 regaleira.pt

Built between 1904 and 1910, this palace and its extensive gardens are a feast of historical and religious references, occult symbols and mystery. The brainchild of eccentric millionaire António Augusto Carvalho Monteiro, the grounds are riddled with secret passages and hidden tunnels. Sintra's local government reclaimed the site as a national monument in 1997 and opened it to the public shortly afterwards.

→

Spiral Initiation Wells at the Quinta da Regaleira

PALÁCIO NACIONAL DE SINTRA

📍 Largo Rainha Dona Amélia 🕐 Mar–late Oct: 9:30am–7pm daily; Nov–early Mar: 9:30am–6pm daily (last adm 30 mins before closing) 🚫 1 Jan, 25 Dec 🌐 parquesdesintra.pt

One of the best-preserved royal palaces in Portugal, Sintra's National Palace has a fascinating mix of Moorish and Manueline architecture. Inside, the lavishly decorated, whimsically themed rooms are a delight to explore.

At the heart of the old town of Sintra (Sintra Vila), a pair of strange conical chimneys rise above the Royal Palace. The main part of the palace, including this central block with its plain Gothic façade, was built by João I in the late 14th century, on a site once occupied by the Moorish rulers. The Paço Real, as it is also known, soon became the favourite summer retreat for the court, and continued as a residence for Portuguese royalty until 1910. Additions to the building by Manuel I, in the early 16th century, echo the Moorish style. The palace stretches across a number of levels, in acquiescence to the mountain on which it sits.

The Sala dos Brasões, one of Europe's most impressive heraldry rooms.

Did You Know?

Afonso VI was imprisoned by his brother, Pedro II, in the palace for nine years.

Sala das Galés (galleons)

Jardim da Preta, a walled garden

Quarto de Dom Sebastião, the bedroom of the young king.

← The white walls and distinctive chimneys of the Palácio Nacional de Sintra

Sala das Sereias, or Room of the Sirens

Sala Árabe, decorated with fine azulejos

The kitchens, where royal banquets were once prepared, sit beneath the huge conical chimneys.

Moorish-style windows on the Ala Manuelina

Entrance

Sala dos Archeiros, the entrance hall

↑ Sintra's national palace, showcasing an intriguing meld of architectural styles

SINTRA: PALÁCIO NACIONAL DA PENA

Manuel II's bedroom, an oval-shaped room decorated with a stuccoed ceiling.

🏠 Estrada da Pena, 5 km (3 miles) S of Sintra 🚌 434 from Avenida Dr Miguel Bombarda, Sintra ⏰ Mar–late Oct: 9:45am–7pm daily; Nov–early Mar: 10am–6pm daily 🚫 1 Jan, 25 Dec 🌐 parquesdesintra.pt

On the highest peaks of the Serra de Sintra stands the spectacular palace of Pena. Built in the 19th century for Queen Maria II's flamboyantly creative husband, Ferdinand Saxe-Coburg-Gotha, it comprises an eclectic medley of architectural styles.

The bright pink-and-yellow walls of the palace stand over the ruins of a Hieronymite monastery, founded here in the 15th century. Ferdinand appointed a German architect, Baron Von Eschwege, to build his dream summer palace, filled with international oddities and surrounded by a park. Construction started in 1840, and the extravagant project would ultimately last 45 years – the rest of the king's life. With the declaration of the Republic in 1910, the palace became a museum, preserved as it was when the royal family lived here.

FERDINAND: KING CONSORT

Born a German prince, Ferdinand was known in Portugal as Dom Fernando II, the "artist" king. Like his cousin Prince Albert, who married the English Queen Victoria, he loved art, nature and new inventions of the time. He was himself a watercolour painter. Ferdinand enthusiastically adopted his new country and devoted his life to patronizing the arts. In 1869, 16 years after the death of Maria II, Ferdinand married his mistress, the opera singer Countess Edla. His long-held dream of building the astonishing palace at Pena was finally completed in 1885, the year he died.

Kitchen, where the dinner service still bears Ferdinand's coat of arms.

The Romanticist Palácio Nacional da Pena, located in the hills of Sintra ↑

The Triton Arch, encrusted with Neo-Manueline decoration

Arab Room

The cloister, part of the original monastery buildings and decorated with colourful tiles

Great Hall

Entrance

Entrance arch, a studded archway topped with crenellated turrets

→ The brightly painted hilltop palace is a UNESCO World Heritage Site

PALÁCIO NACIONAL DE QUELUZ

🏛 Largo do Palácio, Queluz; 14 km (9 miles) NW of Lisbon
🚌 From Lisbon (Colégio Militar) 🚃 Queluz-Belas or Queluz-Massama ⏰ Mar-late Oct: 9am-7pm daily (last adm 1 hr before closing); Nov-early Mar: 9am-5:30pm daily (last adm 30 mins before closing) 🚫 1 Jan, 25 Dec 🌐 parquesdesintra.pt

Often referred to as Lisbon's Versailles, this palace is an excellent example of 18th-century Portuguese architecture. Initially intended as a summer residence, the royal family lived here permanently from 1794 until their departure for Brazil in 1807.

In 1747, Pedro, younger son of João V, commissioned Mateus Vicente to transform his 17th-century hunting lodge into a Rococo summer palace. The central section, including a music room and chapel, was built first, and after Pedro's marriage in 1760 to the future Maria I, the palace was again extended. The French architect Jean-Baptiste Robillion added the sumptuous Robillion Pavilion and gardens, cleared space for the throne room and redesigned the music room. During Maria's reign, the royal family kept a menagerie and went boating on the *azulejo*-lined canal.

Sala dos Embaixadores

The Lion Staircase, gracefully linking the lower gardens to the palace.

Shell waterfall

Don Quixote chamber, the royal bedroom, with its domed ceiling and magnificent floor.

The flamboyant, Rococo-style Robillion Pavilion.

Did You Know?

Dom Pedro IV was born and died in the Quixote chamber, despite living most of his life in Brazil.

The royal family's living rooms and bedrooms, which opened out onto the Malta Gardens.

Chapel

Neptune's Fountain

Music room, where Maria I's orchestra performed operas and concerts.

Throne room

Entrance

Malta Gardens

The Hanging Gardens, elaborately designed by Robillion and built over arches.

↑ The palace and its carefully arranged formal gardens

MARIA I (1734-1816)

Maria, the eldest daughter of José I, lived at Queluz palace after her marriage to her uncle, Pedro. Serious and devout, Maria was a conscientious queen, but suffered increasingly from bouts of melancholia. When her son José died from smallpox in 1788, she went hopelessly mad. Visitors to Queluz were dismayed by her agonizing shrieks as she suffered visions and hallucinations. After the 1807 invasion, her younger son João took Maria to Brazil.

EXPERIENCE MORE

Palácio de Mafra

📍 Terreiro de Dom
João V, Mafra 🚌 From
Lisbon Ⓜ Campo
Grande, then 🚌 Ericeira
🕐 9:30am–5:30pm Wed–
Mon (last adm 4:45pm)
📅 1 Jan, Easter, 1 May,
24 & 25 Dec 🌐 palacio
mafra.gov.pt

This massive Baroque palace and monastery were built during the reign of João V, and began with a vow by the young king to build a new monastery and basilica, supposedly in return for an heir. Work began in 1717 on a modest project but, as wealth began to pour into the royal coffers from Brazil, the king and his Italian-trained architect, Johann Friedrich Ludwig (1670–1752), made ever more extravagant plans. No expense was spared: the finished project housed 330 friars, a royal palace and one of the finest libraries in Europe, decorated with precious marble, exotic wood and countless works of art. The magnificent basilica was consecrated on the king's 41st birthday, 22 October 1730.

The palace was only popular with those members of the royal family who enjoyed hunting deer and wild boar. Most of the finest furniture and art works were taken to Brazil when the royal family escaped the French invasion in 1807. The monastery was abandoned in 1834 following the dissolution of all religious orders, and the palace itself was abandoned in 1910.

The tour starts in the rooms of the monastery, through the pharmacy, with some alarming medical instruments, to the hospital, where patients could see and hear Mass in the adjoining chapel from their beds. Upstairs, the sumptuous state rooms extend across the whole of the west façade, with the king's apartments at one end and the queen's apartments at the other. Midway, the long, imposing façade is relieved by the twin towers of the domed basilica. The church's interior is decorated in contrasting colours of marble and furnished with six early 19th-century organs. Mafra's greatest treasure, however, is its library, with its Rococo-style wooden bookcases and a collection of over 40,000 books in gold-embossed leather bindings, including a prized first edition of *Os Lusíadas* (1572) by the Portuguese poet, Luís de Camões (1524–80).

1717

Construction of the Palácio de Mafra began, a project so ambitious it almost bankrupted the state.

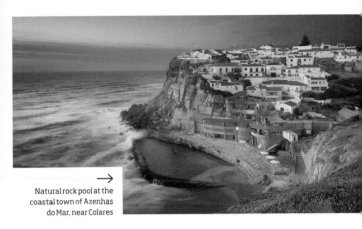

→ Natural rock pool at the coastal town of Azenhas do Mar, near Colares

Colares
📱 🅸 Cabo da Roca;
219 280 081

On the lower slopes of the Serra de Sintra, this lovely village faces the sea over a green valley. A leafy avenue winds its way up to the village. Small quantities of the famous Colares wine are still made. The hardy vines grow in sandy soil, with the roots set deep in clay; these were among the few vines in Europe to survive the disastrous phylloxera epidemic brought from America in the late 19th

← The impressive Baroque façade of the Palácio de Mafra

century. The insect ate the vines' roots but could not penetrate the dense sandy soil of the Atlantic coast. The Adega Regional de Colares on Alameda de Coronel Linhares de Lima offers wine tastings.

There are several popular beach resorts west of Colares. Just north of Praia das Maçãs is the picturesque village of Azenhas do Mar, clinging to the cliffs; to the south is the larger resort of Praia Grande.

Estoril
📱 🚉 🅸 Largo de Camões,
Cascais; 912 034 214

The lovely resort town of Estoril is a tourist and business resort, and a place

for comfortable retirement. What separates Estoril from Cascais, besides a pleasant beach promenade of 3 km (2 miles) and a mansion-covered ridge known as Monte Estoril, is its sense of place. The heart of Estoril is immediately accessible from the train station. On one side of the tracks is the riviera-like, but relaxed beach; on the other a palm-lined park flanked by grand buildings, stretching up past fountains to a casino.

Dwarfing the casino is the Estoril Congress Centre, a vast multipurpose edifice that speaks confidently of Estoril's contemporary role

Ericeira

🚌 🚆 ℹ️ **Rua Dr Eduardo Burnay 46; 261 863 122**

Ericeira is an old fishing village that keeps its traditions despite an ever-increasing influx of summer visitors who enjoy the bracing climate, clean, sandy beaches and fresh seafood. In July and August, pavement cafés, restaurants and bars around the tree-lined Praça da República are buzzing late into the night. Alternative attractions include Santa Marta park and a history museum (closed until 2020).

The unspoilt old town, a maze of whitewashed houses and narrow, cobbled streets, is perched high above the ocean. From Largo das Ribas, at the top of a 30-m (100-ft) stone-faced cliff, there is a bird's-eye view over the busy fishing harbour below, where tractors haul the

boats out of reach of the tide. In mid-August, the annual fishermen's festival is celebrated with a candle-lit procession to the harbour at the foot of the cliffs for the blessing of the boats.

On 5 October 1910, Manuel II, the last king of Portugal, sailed into exile from Ericeira as the Republic was declared in Lisbon; a tiled panel in the fishermen's chapel of Santo António above the harbour records the event. The banished king settled in Twickenham, southwest London, where he died in 1932.

Monserrate

🚗 **Rua Barbosa du Bocage** 🚉 **To Sintra, then taxi or bus 435** 🕐 **Late Mar-late Oct: 9:30am-8pm daily (to 7pm for the palace); late Oct-late Mar: 10am-6pm daily (to 5pm for the palace)** 🚫 **1 Jan, 25 Dec** 🌐 **parquesde sintra.pt**

The wild, romantic garden of this once magnificent estate is full of exotic trees and flowering shrubs. Among the subtropical foliage and valley of tree ferns are a small lake and a

chapel, built as a ruin, tangled in the roots of a giant *Ficus* tree. Its history dates back to the Moors but it takes its name from a small 16th-century chapel dedicated to Our Lady of Montserrat in Catalonia, Spain. The gardens were landscaped in the late 1700s by a wealthy young Englishman, William Beckford. They were later immortalized by Lord Byron in *Childe Harold's Pilgrimage* (1812).

In 1856, the abandoned estate was bought by another Englishman, Sir Francis Cook, who built a fantastic Moorish-style palace (which has been restored) and transformed the gardens with a large lawn, camellias and subtropical trees from all over the world.

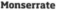

← The Palace of Monserrate's beautifully wrought Romantic architecture, inside and out

← Bathers enjoying the clear blue waters and sandy beach at Cascais

Cascais

 Largo de Camões; 912 094 314

A holiday resort for well over a century, Cascais possesses a certain illustriousness that younger resorts lack. Its history is visible in its villas, summer residences of wealthy Lisboetas who followed King Luís I's lead during the late 19th century.

Cascais today is a favoured suburb of Lisbon, a place of seaside apartments and pine-studded plots by golf courses. But the beautiful coastline beyond the town has been left largely undeveloped.

Housed in a castle-like villa, the Museu Condes de Castro Guimarães is the best place to get a taste of Cascais's history.

The Casa das Histórias Paula Rego is dedicated to the work of the painter, illustrator and printmaker.

Costa da Caparica

To Cacilhas or Trafaria then bus To Pragal then bus **Frente Urbana de Praias; 212 900 071**

Long beaches backed by sand dunes make this a popular holiday resort for Lisboetas, who come to swim, sunbathe and enjoy the beach cafés and seafood restaurants. A railway with open carriages runs for 10 km (6 miles) along the coast in summer.

The first beaches reached from the town are popular with families with children, while the furthest beaches suit those seeking quiet isolation.

EAT

O Pescador

This nautical-themed eatery is lined with wooden tables and fishing paraphernalia. Diners can sit on the pleasant outdoor terrace and enjoy the menu's emphasis on fresh fish.

Rua das Flores 10b, Cascais **Wed** **restaurante pescador.com**

€€€

Saudade

An appealing café and art gallery near the train station that serves coffees, cakes, sandwiches and *petiscos* (Portuguese tapas).

Avenida Dr Miguel Bombarda 6, Sintra **212 428 804**

€€€

Palmela

🏰 🚌 ℹ️ **Castelo de Palmela; 212 332 122**

The formidable castle at Palmela stands over the small hill town, high on a northeastern spur of the wooded Serra da Arrábida. Its strategic position dominates the plain for miles around, especially when floodlit at night. Heavily defen-ded by the Moors, it was finally conquered in the 12th century and given by Sancho I to the Knights of the Order of Santiago. In 1423, João I transformed the castle into a monastery for the Order. It has since been restored and converted into a splendid *pousada*, with a restaurant in the monks' refectory and a swimming pool for residents, hidden inside the castle walls. From the castle terraces and the top of the 14th-century keep, there are fantastic views over the Serra da Arrábida to the south and across the Tagus to Lisbon. In the town square below, the church of São Pedro contains 18th-century tiles of scenes from St Peter's life.

The annual wine festival, the Festa das Vindimas, is held on the first weekend of September in front of the 17th-century Paços do Concelho (town hall). On the final day of celebrations there is a spectacular firework display from the castle walls.

↑ The castle at Palmela with views over the Serra da Arrábida

Serra da Arrábida

🚌 **From Setúbal**
ℹ️ **Parque Natural da Arrábida, Praça da República, Setúbal; 265 541 140**

The Serra da Arrábida Natural Park covers the range of limestone mountains that stretches east–west along the coast between Sesimbra and Setúbal. It was established to protect the wild, beautiful landscape and rich variety of birds and wildlife, including wildcats and badgers.

The sheltered, south-facing slopes are thickly covered with aromatic and evergreen shrubs and trees, such as cypress and pine, more typical of the Mediterranean. Vineyards also thrive on the sheltered slopes and the town of Vila Nogueira de Azeitão is particularly known for its wine, Moscatel de Setúbal. The Estrada de Escarpa (the N379-1) snakes across the top of the ridge and affords astounding views. A narrow road winds down to Portinho da Arrábida, a sheltered cove with a beach of fine white sand and crystal clear sea, popular with underwater fishermen. The sandy beaches of Galapos and Figueirinha are a little further east along the coast road towards Setúbal. Just east of Sesimbra, the Serra da Arrábida drops to the sea in the sheer 380-m (1,250-ft) cliffs of Risco, the highest in mainland Portugal.

→

Jetty with fishing boats moored on the mud flats at Carrasqueira

Alcácer do Sal

🏛 🚌 *i* Largo Luís de Camões; 911 794 685

Bypassed by the main road, the ancient town of Alcácer do Sal (*al-kasr* from the Arabic for castle, and *do sal* from its trade in salt) sits peacefully on the north bank of the Sado river.

The imposing castle was a hillfort as early as the 6th century BC. The Phoenicians made an inland trading port here, and the castle later became a Roman stronghold. Rebuilt by the Moors, it was conquered by Afonso II in 1217. The buildings have now taken on a new life as a *pousada*, with views over the rooftops. Also notable here is the Cripta Arqueológica do Castelo, an archaeological museum holding locally excavated items. The collections include artifacts from the Iron Age, as well as from the Roman, Moorish and medieval periods.

There are pleasant cafés along the riverside promenade and several historic churches.

Alcochete

🚌 *i* Largo da Misericórdia; 212 348 655

This delightful old town overlooks the Tagus estuary from the southern shore. Salt has long been one of the main industries here, and saltpans can still be seen north and south of the town, while in the town centre a large statue of a muscular salt worker has the inscription: "Do Sal a Revolta e a Esperança" (From Salt to Rebellion and Hope).

The Reserva Natural do Estuário do Tejo covers a vast area of estuary water, salt marshes and small islands around Alcochete, and is a very important breeding ground for water birds.

Península de Tróia

🚌 🚢 Tróia *i* Tróia Resort; 265 499 400
🕐 Cetóbriga: Mar–Oct: 10am–1pm, 2:30–6pm Wed–Sun (to 6:30pm Jun–Aug)

Holiday apartments dominate the tip of the Tróia Peninsula, easily accessible from Setúbal by ferry. The Atlantic coast, stretching south for 18 km (11 miles) of untouched sandy beaches, is now the haunt of sun-seekers in the summer.

Near Tróia, in the sheltered lagoon, the Roman town of Cetóbriga was the site of a thriving fish-salting business; the stone tanks and ruined buildings are open to visit.

Further on, Carrasqueira is an old fishing community where you can still see traditional reed houses, with walls and roofs made from thatch.

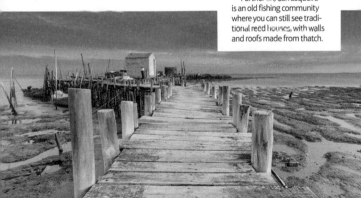

Sesimbra

🏛 ℹ Rua da Fortaleza de Santiago; 212 288 540

Protected from north winds by the slopes of the Serra da Arrábida, this busy fishing village has become a popular holiday resort. The old town is a maze of steep narrow streets, with the Santiago Fort (now a customs post) in the centre overlooking the sea. From the terrace there are views of the town, the Atlantic and the wide sandy beach that stretches out on either side.

Sesimbra is fast developing as a resort, with plentiful pavement cafés and bars that are always busy on sunny days.

The fishing fleet is moored in the Porto do Abrigo to the west of the main town. The harbour is reached by taking Avenida dos Náufragos, a sweeping promenade that follows the beach out of town. When the fishing boats return from a day at sea, a colourful, noisy fish auction takes place on the quayside. The day's catch can be tasted in the town's excellent fish restaurants along the shore.

High above the town is the Moorish castle, greatly restored in the 18th century when a church and small flower-filled cemetery were added nside the walls. There are wonderful views from the ramparts, especially at sunset.

Cabo Espichel

🏛 From Sesimbra

Sheer cliffs drop straight into the sea on this windswept promontory. The Romans named it Promontorium Barbaricum, alluding to its dangerous location, and a lighthouse warns sailors of the treacherous rocks below. Stunning views of the ocean and the coast can be enjoyed from this bleak outcrop of land but beware of the strong gusts of wind on the cliff edge. In this desolate setting is the impressive Santuário de Nossa Senhora do Cabo, a late-17th-century church with its back to the sea. On either side of the church, a long line of pilgrims' lodgings, facing inwards, form an open courtyard. Baroque paintings, *ex votos* and a frescoed ceiling decorate the church's interior. Nearby, a domed chapel has tiled blue-and-white *azulejo* panels depicting fishing scenes. The site became a popular place of pilgrimage in the 13th century when a local man had a vision of the Madonna rising from the sea on a mule. Legend has it that the mule tracks can be seen embedded in the rock.

↓ Brightly painted fishing boats moored in the harbour at Sesimbra

Setúbal

🏛️🚌🚆 ℹ️ **Casa da Baía, Ave Luísa Todi 468; 265 545 010**

An important industrial town and the third-largest port in Portugal (after Lisbon and Porto), Setúbal makes a good base from which to explore the area. To the south of the central gardens and fountains are the fishing harbour, marina and ferry port, and a lively covered market. North of the gardens is the old town, with attractive pedestrian streets and squares full of cafés.

The 16th-century cathedral, dedicated to Santa Maria da Graça, has glorious 18th-century tiled panels, and gilded altar decoration. Street names commemorate two famous Setúbal residents: Manuel Barbosa du Bocage (1765–1805), whose satirical poetry landed him in prison, and Luísa Todi (1753–1833), a celebrated opera singer.

In Roman times, fish-salting was the most important industry here. Rectangular stone tanks used for this process can still be seen on Travessa Frei Gaspar.

To the north of the old town, the striking Igreja de Jesus (currently closed for restoration) is one of Setúbal's treasures. Designed by the architect Diogo Boitac in 1494, the lofty interior is adorned with twisted columns, of pinkish Arrábida limestone and rope-like stone ribs, recognized as the first examples of the Manueline style.

On Rua do Balneário, in the old monastic quarters, a museum houses 14 remarkable paintings of the life of Christ. The works are attributed to followers of the Renaissance painter Jorge Afonso (1520–30).

The Museu de Arqueologia e Etnografia displays a wealth of finds from digs around Setúbal, including Bronze Age pots and Roman coins. The ethnography display shows local arts, crafts and industries, including the processing of salt and cork over the centuries.

The star-shaped Castelo de São Filipe was built in 1595 by Philip II of Spain during the period of Spanish rule to keep a wary eye on pirates, English invaders and the local population. It now houses a boutique hotel, but the battlements and ramparts are open to the public and offer marvellous views over the city and the Sado estuary.

Setúbal is an ideal starting point for a tour by car of the unspoilt Reserva Natural do Estuário do Sado, a vast stretch of mud flats, shallow lagoons and salt marshes, which has been explored and inhabited since 3500 BC.

EAT

O Barbas Catedral

This renowned restaurant, which overlooks the breakers of Caparica beach, is usually packed at weekends thanks to its delicious seafood dishes.

📍 **Apoio de Praia 13, Caparica**
📞 212 900 163

O Galeão

Expect sparkling sea views from the terrace, great salads and fresh fish at this restaurant above the water.

📍 **Portinho da Arrábida**
📞 212 180 533

Ribamar

This upmarket restaurant is right on the seafront, and has been serving tasty seafood dishes for over 60 years.

📍 **Avenida dos Náufragos 29, Sesimbra** 🌐 ribamar.pt

BEFORE YOU GO

Forward planning is essential for any successful trip. Prepare yourself for any eventuality by brushing up on the following points before you set off.

AT A GLANCE

CURRENCY
Euro (EUR)

AVERAGE DAILY SPEND

SAVE	SPEND	SPLURGE
€35	€70	€150+

Bottled Water €0.80	Coffee €1	Beer €3	Dinner for Two €45

ESSENTIAL PHRASES

Hello	Olá
Thank you	Obrigado/Obrigada
Please	Por favor
Goodbye	Adeus
Do you speak English	Fala inglês?
I don't understand	Não compreendo

ELECTRICITY SUPPLY
Power sockets are type F, fitting a two-prong plug. Standard voltage is 220-240v.

Passports and Visas

EU nationals may visit for an unlimited period, registering with local authorities after 3 months. Citizens of the US, Canada, Australia and New Zealand can reside without a visa for up to 90 days. For those arriving from other countries, check with your local Portuguese embassy or on the **Camara Municipal website**.
Camara Municipal
[w] cm-lisboa.pt/en

Travel Safety Advice

Visitors can get up-to-date travel safety information from the **UK Foreign and Commonwealth Department**, the **US State Department** and the **Australian Department of Foreign Affairs and Trade**.
AUS
[w] smartraveller.gov.au
UK
[w] gov.uk/foreign-travel-advice
US
[w] travel.state.gov

Customs Information

An individual is permitted to carry the following within the EU for personal use:
Tobacco products 800 cigarettes, 400 cigarillos, 200 cigars or 1 kg of smoking tobacco.
Alcohol 10 litres of alcoholic beverages above 22% strength, 20 litres of alcoholic beverages below 22% strength, 90 litres of wine (60 litres of which can be sparkling wine) and 110 litres of beer.
Cash If you plan to enter or leave the EU with €10,000 or more in cash (or the equivalent in other currencies) you must declare it to the customs authorities.

Language

English is widely spoken in Portugal's cities, but the Portuguese are proud of their language and appreciate visitors' efforts to communicate. While written Portuguese is similar to Spanish, the idiosyncratic pronunciation of spoken Portuguese can demand several attempts to correctly enunciate even simple phrases. Attempting to communicate solely in Spanish may cause offence.

Insurance

It is wise to take out an insurance policy covering theft, loss of belongings, medical problems, cancellations and delays. EU citizens are eligible for free emergency medical care in Portugal provided they have a valid **EHIC** (European Health Insurance Card).
EHIC.
w gov.uk/european-health-insurance-card

Vaccinations

No inoculations are necessary for Portugal.

Booking Accommodation

Lisbon offers a variety of accommodation, ranging from boutique hotels to campsites, budget hostels to private apartment rentals. A list of accommodation can be found on the **Visit Portugal** website. During the summer months, lodgings are snapped up fast and prices become inflated, so book in advance. Lisbon is a popular short city-break destination, and it can also be difficult to find a last-minute weekend booking during the low season (Dec–Mar). Visitors to Lisbon are required to pay a €1/night city tourism tax for stays up to 7 days, which is payable on top of your bill. Children below the age of 13 are exempt. Hotels are required by law to share details of foreign visitors with the local authorities.

Visit Portugal
w visitportugal.com

Money

Most establishments accept major credit, debit and prepaid currency cards. Contactless payments are gradually becoming more common in Lisbon, but it's always a good idea to carry cash for smaller items like coffee and pastéis de nata, or when visiting markets. ATMs are widely available across the city.

Travellers with Specific Needs

Lisbon's hills can prove a challenge to navigate for wheelchair-users and those with prams. Facilities in Lisbon have improved over recent years, with wheelchairs, adapted toilets, and reserved car parking available at the airports and main stations. Ramps and lifts are installed in many public places and some buses (marked with a blue-and-white logo at the front) accommodate wheelchair-users. Tour companies, such as **Tourism For All,** offer specialist holiday packages, while **Accessible Portugal** gives comprehensive advice on travelling with limited mobility.
Accessible Portugal
w accessibleportugal.com
Tourism For All
w tourism-for-all.com

Closures

Lunchtime Some museums and public buildings may close from noon until 2pm.

Monday State-run museums, public buildings and monuments are closed all day.

Sunday Churches and cathedrals are closed to tourists during Mass. Some public transport runs less frequently.

Public holidays Most museums, public buildings and many shops close early or for the day.

GETTING AROUND

Whether exploring Lisbon by foot or public transport, here is everything you need to know to navigate the city like a pro.

AT A GLANCE

PUBLIC TRANSPORT COSTS

METRO

€1.45

1 hour transfers included

BUS

€1.80

single journey on bus

TRAM

€2.85

single journey on tram

SPEED LIMIT

MOTORWAY

120 km/h (75mph)

DUAL CARRIAGEWAY

100 km/h (60mph)

SECONDARY ROAD

90 km/h (55mph)

URBAN AREAS

50 km/h (30mph)

Arriving by Air

Lisbon Humberto Delgado Airport is served by local and international flights and has excellent transport links to the city centre. **Lisbon Humberto Delgado Airport** W ana.pt

Train Travel

International Train Travel
There are two main routes into Portugal by train. The famous Sud Express train, which departs daily at 6:45pm from Irun on the French-Spanish border, can be reached from Austerlitz station in Paris. Travelling from London to Lisbon, using the **Eurostar** to reach Paris, and then the Sud Express to Lisbon, takes approximately 30 hours. Alternatively, the overnight train from Madrid takes 10 hours. Both routes are operated by the Spanish state-run service **Renfe.** You can purchase tickets online or at Lisbon's international train stations. It is sensible to book ahead in peak season (Jul–Aug).
Eurostar W eurostar.com; **Renfe** W renfe.com

Regional Trains
CP (Comboios de Portugal) is the country's national rail operator. Most parts of Portugal are served by rail, although the more remote lines have sadly been made obsolete by new road links. Lisbon has four main train stations: Rossio, Cais do Sodré, Santa Apolónia and Oriente. Rossio and Cais do Sodré cover local journeys with lines to Sintra and Cascais, respectively. Santa Apolónia and Oriente provide links to international destinations and those across Portugal, like Porto and Coimbra. All trains should be pre-booked either online or at the station, except for journeys on urban rail networks (*urbanas*), such as the Sintra and Cascais lines. A conductor will validate tickets on-board and will often ask for ID. Tickets for *urbanas* can be bought at the station prior to

departure and should be validated at the ticket machines on the platform before boarding.
CP W cp.pt

Public Transport

State-owned **Carris** is Lisbon's main public transport authority and is responsible for buses, trams and elevators. The metro is run separately, also by the state. Timetables, ticket information, maps and more can be found online, on the Carris app and inside some metro stations.
Carris W carris.pt

Tickets
Single-trip paper tickets for buses, trams and funiculars can be bought upon boarding. Multi-trip paper tickets have been replaced with electronic passes, such as the tourist-friendly **Viva Viagem** smart card. This "Zapping" card costs €0.50 and each traveller must have their own. They can be purchased at vending machines and ticket offices in metro stations across the city, including Cais do Sodré and Marquês de Pombal, and some railway stations, shops and newsagents. Buying a pre-paid Viva Viagem is the most practical option for visitors, as you can top up your card's balance whenever necessary, travelling across the Carris and metro networks at a lower price. You can also load Viva Viagem cards with a 24-hour pass, which allows unlimited travel with Carris and on the metro for €6.30. Passes that include the Tagus ferries (€9.35) or Sintra and Cascais train lines (€10.40) are also available. Note that the balance remaining on the card cannot be refunded.
Viva Viagem W portalviva.pt

Metro
The fastest and cheapest way to get around town is by the **Metropolitano de Lisboa**. Metro stations are signposted with a red M, and the service operates from 6:30am to 1am every day. There are currently over 50 metro stations operating on four lines. These lines link the metro to major bus, train and ferry services, and provide transport from Lisbon's suburbs

to the city centre. Although the metro can be very busy during rush hour, there are frequent trains. The system is safe to travel on by night, since police regularly patrol the stations and trains. All stations have automatic gates at the entrance to the platform and a valid ticket must be passed over the electronic scanner when entering and leaving the station.
Metropolitano de Lisboa W metrolisboa.pt

Trams and Funiculars
Trams are a pleasant ways of sightseeing in Lisbon but they only operate in limited areas of the city, along the river to Belém and around the hillier parts of Lisbon. At €2.85 for a single trip without a Viva Viagem card, they can be a costly choice. The charming, pre-World War I models still run alongside new trams with sleek interiors. Perhaps the most popular route is tram 28, which passes by Alfama and Mouraria as it circumvents Castelo de São Jorge, before taking a scenic route across the city to the more grandiose districts of São Bento and Estrela. Three historic funiculars (Gloria, Bica and Lavra) carry weary Lisboetas up several of the city's steepest hills, and are classed as national monuments. Similarly, the Elevador de Santa Justa is a useful and enjoyable tourist experience, but queues can be long. Purchase a Viva Viagem card to minimize the cost of trams, funiculars and the Elevador de Santa Justa.

Buses
The bus network is Lisbon's most extensive public transport system, and buses go just about everywhere. They are usually yellow and are a bright feature around the city's streets, generally running from 5:30am to 1am in the inner city. A small number of night services continue outside these hours. The bus timetable suffers from Lisbon's traffic problems, which means that you sometimes have to wait a long time to board a very crowded bus. Bus stops are indicated by a sign marked Paragem and display the routes that serve them, along with timetables. Many stops and buses now also display real-time schedule information.

Long-Distance Bus Travel

Sete Rios is Lisbon's main bus station and there are several private companies operating coach services. **Rede Expressos** covers most of Portugal, linking Braga, Porto, Lisbon and Faro. As a general rule, you can no longer buy tickets on-board for long distance trips. There are discounts for booking early, either online or in bus stations at the relevant company's kiosk. Tickets for shorter trips, however, must be bought at the station or from the driver. **TST** serves destinations south of the Tagus. Buses leave from Praça de Espanha for destinations such as Costa da Caparica (1 hr) and Sesimbra (1 hr 45 mins). **EVA** covers the Algarve particularly well and is based at the Sete Rios bus terminal.

EVA 🌐 eva-bus.com; **Rede Expressos** 🌐 rede-expressos.pt/en; **TST** 🌐 tsuldotejo.pt

Boats and Ferries

The frequent commuter ferries over the Tagus river, which depart roughly every 15 minutes, make for a pleasant excursion to the port suburb of Cacilhas. Most ferry services on the Tagus are run by **Transtejo** and depart regularly from Cais do Sodré, Terreiro do Paço and Belém to several destinations south of the river. Trips generally last 15–25 minutes and are worth making purely for the fabulous views of Lisbon.

Transtejo 🌐 transtejo.pt

Trips and Tours

There are two main hop-on hop-off tour bus operators in Lisbon although, due to the inner city's hilly nature, bus routes mostly follow the city's flatter outskirts, past sights such as the Torre de Belém, Basilica da Estrela and Parque Eduardo VII. Trips on the red **City Sightseeing** buses cost around €22, with a choice of two routes through the east or west of the city. For a similar price, state-run **Carristur**'s yellow bus routes include a tour along the Tagus. Tickets for both companies are valid for 24 hours and can be purchased online or on-board. Tuk-tuks, which are well suited to navigating the inner city and provide

a more personalized, often exciting (or nerve-wracking) experience, have become popular in recent years. **Eco Tuk Tuk Lisbon** provides tours from around €70 for 1 hour. Alternatively you can haggle with the drivers lining the streets next to Sé Cathedral. There is a large choice of tour operators offering trips of varying lengths to other cities in Portugal. Day trips from Lisbon include destinations like Sintra, Cabo da Roca and Cascais, or Arrábida's rugged coastline. Tours can be booked directly with the operator, through a travel agent and at some hotels.

Carristur 🌐 carris.pt/en/carristur
City Sightseeing 🌐 city-sightseeing.com
Eco Tuk Tuk Lisbon 🌐 ecotuktours.com

Taxis

Taxis in Lisbon are relatively inexpensive compared to the rest of Europe and can work out cheaper than public transport for large groups. Most drivers only accept cash and can be hailed in the street and at taxi ranks. A green light indicates that the taxi is available and two green lights mean a higher rate. The normal starting rate for a taxi is €3.25 during the day and €3.90 at night. Ensure that the meter is on, suggest agreeing on a price for longer routes and always check the extra cost for luggage before setting off. Two of the largest firms are **Autocoope** and **Radio Taxis**, but taxi apps such as Uber also operate in Lisbon.

Autocoope 🌐 autocoope.pai.pt
Radio Taxis 🌐 taxislisboa.com

Driving

Driving around Lisbon can be a daunting experience, thanks to a complex street plan, traffic jams and scarce parking.

Driving to Lisbon

There are seven roads into Lisbon. Those arriving from the south can cross to central Lisbon via the Ponte 25 de Abril or the newer Ponte Vasco da Gama. From the north, the A1 (E1) motorway brings you to Lisbon's north-eastern outskirts. Those arriving from Cascais and the Lisbon Coast enter via the tolled A5 motorway or the coastal N6 road. Most of the main motorways in Portugal are toll roads, paid electronically. The easiest system to use is **EasyToll**, which matches your credit card to your licence plate and automatically deducts the necessary funds. Payments and details can be managed on their website. If you bring your own foreign-registered car, you must carry a valid driver's licence, proof of ownership, insurance and address, as well as an up-to-date MOT certificate. After 183 days, the car must either be registered in Portugal or taken to another country.

EasyToll 🔳 portugaltolls.com

Driving in Lisbon
City centre streets are narrow, difficult to navigate and often congested. A vast network of ring roads traces the outskirts, although a missed or wrong exit can result in a severe detour. The city offers relatively few on-street parking spaces, but there are many underground car parks, marked by signs with a white P on a blue background. **The European Car Parking Guide** lists car parks around Lisbon. If your car is towed or clamped, contact **EMEL** based in Sete Rios. You will have to pay a fee of up to C300 to retrieve it, as well as pay for the parking violation.

EMEL 🔳 emel.pt ; **The European Car Parking Guide** 🔳 car-parking.eu/portugal/lisbon

Car Rental
Most major car hire companies have offices at the airport. To rent a car in Portugal you must be over 18 and have held a valid driver's licence for at least one year, although those under 25 may need to pay a surcharge. Prices rise considerably in peak season (Jul–Aug) and some companies offer special off-peak (Dec–Mar) and weekend deals. As Lisbon's streets are narrow and Portuguese drivers are infamously erratic, it is sensible to arrange third-party insurance beforehand or take the pricier "no excess" insurance deals offered upon pick-up. Most car hire companies give the option to pay all road toll fees upon the vehicle's return.

Rules of the Road
Drive on the right and use the left lane only for passing. Seat belts are required for all passengers and heavy fines are incurred for using a mobile phone while driving. Drivers are required to stop at pedestrian crossings. The blood-alcohol concentration (BAC) limit is 0.5mg/ml and is very strictly enforced. If you are drinking alcohol, use public transport or a taxi. Always carry your passport, licence and insurance details. In the event of an accident or breakdown, the driver and passengers must don a fluorescent yellow safety vest and erect a collapsible warning triangle 50m behind the vehicle. Both of these items must be stored in the trunk at all times. Driver's licences issued by any EU member state are valid throughout the EU, including Portugal. If visiting from outside the EU, you may need to apply for an International Driving Permit (IDP). The local motoring association, the **ACP** (Automóvel Club de Portugal), has a reciprocal breakdown service with most other international motoring organizations. To qualify, drivers must take out European cover with their own organization. Should you be involved in a road accident, the emergency services number is 112.

ACP 🔳 acp.pt

Scooter Hire

A growing number of companies, including **Lisbon Bike Rentals**, now offer electric bikes. Scooters and motorcycles are a popular choice, particularly for those looking to explore the Lisbon Coast. Most companies require a deposit and ask that you leave your passport at the rental shop. You must have a driver's licence valid for your desired bike category. Note that 50cc vehicles are forbidden on motorways, which includes the Ponte 25 de Abril and Ponte Vasco da Gama. All riders must wear helmets by law, which can be rented from most hire shops. **LX Rent** is reliable and conveniently located where Alfama meets the Tagus, with scooters from €36/day.

Lisbon Bike Rentals 🔳 lisbonbikerentals.com; **LX Rent** 🔳 lxrent.pt

PRACTICAL INFORMATION

A little local know-how goes a long way in Lisbon. Here is all the essential advice and information you will need during your stay.

AT A GLANCE

EMERGENCY NUMBERS

GENERAL EMERGENCY	AMBULANCE
112	**18**

FIRE SERVICE	POLICE
115	**112**

TIME ZONE
CET/CEST
Central European Summer time (CEST) runs end Mar–end Oct

TAP WATER
Tap water in Lisbon is safe to drink.

TIPPING

Waiter	10%
Hotel Porter	€1–2
Housekeeping	€1–2
Concierge	Not expected
Taxi Driver	10%

Personal Security

While crime in Lisbon's centre is very low, pickpockets are common. Take care in crowded tourist areas and on popular tram routes, particularly the 28 and 15. Keep your belongings in a safe place and with you at all times. If you have anything stolen, report the crime within 24 hours to the nearest police station and take ID with you. Get a copy of the crime report to make an insurance claim. There is a police station specifically for tourists at Praça dos Restauradores, beside the tourist office. Contact your embassy if you have your passport stolen, or in the event of a serious crime or accident.

Health

Seek medicinal supplies and advice for minor ailments from pharmacies (farmácias), identifiable by a green cross. Pharmacists can dispense a range of drugs that would normally be available only on prescription in many other countries. Each pharmacy displays a card in the window showing the address of the nearest all-night pharmacy.

Emergency medical care in Portugal is free for all EU citizens. If you have an EHIC, present this as soon as possible. You may have to pay after treatment and reclaim the money later. For visitors coming from outside the EU, payment of hospital and other medical expenses is the patient's responsibility, so it is important to arrange comprehensive medical insurance before travelling.

Smoking, Alcohol and Drugs

Smoking is banned in most enclosed public spaces and is a fineable offence, although some bars still allow it. Portugal has a high alcohol consumption rate, however it is frowned upon to be openly drunk. It is common for Lisboetas to drink on the street outside the bar of purchase.

All drugs are decriminalized in Portugal, but possession of small quantities is considered a public health issue and results in a warning or small fine. Drug-dealers brazenly plying their wares in the city centre can be a small nuisance.

ID

By law you must carry identification with you at all times. A photocopy of your passport should suffice. If stopped by the police you may be asked to report to a police station with the original document.

Local Customs

Lisbon is a tolerant and open-minded city, but as the pressure of tourism grows, small efforts to integrate are increasingly appreciated. If possible, use simple Portuguese phrases and greetings appropriate to the time of day. A much-loved aspect of Portugal is the slow pace of life. This is evident as a pedestrian, at public events and when making social engagements, so try to stifle any impatience and readjust your tempo suitably.

Visiting Churches and Cathedrals

Most churches and cathedrals will not permit visitors during Sunday Mass. Generally, entrance to churches is free, however a fee may apply to enter special areas, like cloisters. Portugal retains a strong Catholic identity. When visiting religious buildings ensure that you are dressed modestly, with knees and shoulders covered.

Mobile Phones and Wi-Fi

Free Wi-Fi is not yet widespread in Portugal, but it can be found in some restaurants and bars, specifically those aimed at tourists. Visitors travelling to Portugal with EU tariffs are able to use their devices abroad without being affected by roaming charges. Users will be charged the same rates for data, calls and texts as at home.

Post

The postal service is run by **CTT** (Correios de Portugal), which offers a wide range of services at prices lower than the European average. Stamps are sold in post offices, newsagents and on the CTT website. Post should take around 3–5 days to reach the rest of Europe, 7 days for elsewhere in the world and can be tracked on the **CTT** website, where you can also find details of your nearest post office. There is also a choice of international couriers.
CTT
W ctt.pt

Taxes and Refunds

VAT is usually 23 per cent. Under certain conditions, non-EU citizens can claim a rebate. Either claim the rebate before you buy (show your passport to the shop assistant and complete a form) or claim it retrospectively by presenting a customs officer with your receipts as you leave.

Discount Cards

If you plan to pack a lot of sightseeing into a short trip, purchasing an official **Lisboa Card** can be a cost-efficient choice. For €19, adults receive 24 hours of free public transport, which includes the train lines to Cascais and Sintra; free entry to 26 museums and points of interest; and discounts relating to tours, shopping and nightlife. Cards lasting 48 and 72 hours are also available (€32/€40). The cards can be bought online, at the airport and in the tourist information offices at Praça do Comércio and Praça dos Restauradores.
Lisboa Card
W lisboacard.org

INDEX

ACKNOWLEDGMENTS

Dorling Kindersley would like to extend special thanks to the following people for their contribution: Anamika Bhandari, Syed Mohammad Farhan, Shanker Prasad.

The publisher would like to thank the following for their kind permission to reproduce their photographs:

Key: a-above; b-below/bottom; c-centre; f-far; l-left; r-right; t-top

123RF.com: manganganath 41bl; seregalsv 53tr; Michael Spring 79tr.

Michael Abid: 27br.

Alamy Stock Photo: Mauricio Abreu 26tl, 30br; age fotostock / Ken Welsh 73cra; Archive PL 68bl; Art Kowalsky 73tr; John Baran 74br; Bildagentur-online / McPhoto-Boyungs 23tl; Michael Brooks 70crb; Education & Exploration 2 57tr; Education & Exploration 4 23tr; Luis Elvas 16tr; Faraway Photos 71tr; Have Camera Will Travel | Europe 58tr; Peter Herbert 6; Hufton+Crow-VIEW 2t; JeffG

68-9b; Cro Magnon 82; mauritius images GmbH / ClickAlps 97b; Mikehoward 13tl,98b; Roman Pesarenko 80b; Luis Miguel Lopes Pina 93t; Clove Reading 63tr; robertharding / Stuart Black 3tl; Sagaphotos.com / Stephane Gautier 72-3b; M.Sobreira 42bl; Sueddeutsche Zeitung Photo 49cr; Jan Wlodarczyk 22-3b; Dudley Wood 46b.

© Calouste Gulbenkian Foundation, Lisbon: Carlos Azevedo 69tl; Founder's Collection / Catarina Gomes Ferreira 69tr.

Dorling Kindersley: Peter Wilson 16bc.

Dreamstime.com: Allard1 66; Leonid Andronov 55tl; Vichaya Kiatying-Angsulee 29r; Myoung Bae 77b; Dan Grytsku 85br; Miguel Angel Morales Hermo 53cr; Vladimir Korostyshevskiy 59br; Bogdan Lazar 32bl; Mapics 76tr; Juan Moyano 40tl; Roland Nagy 38t; Sean Pavone 84-5t, 87tl; Peek Creative Collective 9br; Carlos

Sanchez Pereyra 10tl; William Perry 78br; Antonio Ribeiro 60-1t; Rosshelen 46-7t; Saiko3p 12bl; Rui G. Santos 81tl; Sohadiszno 24-5b; Stefano Valeri 25tl; Wastesoul 44-5t; Zts 10-1b, 31br, 56br, 62-3bc, 69tl, 92b, 94bl, 96tr.

Getty Images: Mauricio Abreu 36-7b; AWL Images / Mauricio Abreu 34; Corbis Documentary / Sylvain Sonnet 13br; Moment / Gene Krasko 4-5b; Sylvain Sonnet 17b.

iStockphoto.com: e55evu 50; gregobagel 94-5tc; hsvrs 75tr; LordRunar 20; SeanPavonePhoto 14-5bc, 89br; soniabonet 43tl.

©Museu Nacional de Arte Antiga, Lisboa Instituto dos Museus e da Conservação - MC: Paulo Alexandrino 36cb, 37tl, 38bl, 39tl.

Museu do Fado: José Frade 15tr.

SuperStock: Hemis / Pierre Jaques 70b.

For further information see: www.dkimages.com

PHRASE BOOK

IN EMERGENCY

Help!	Socorro!	soo-**koh**-roo
Stop!	Páre!	**pahr'**
Call a doctor!	Chame um médico!	shahm'ooñ **meh**-dee-koo
Call an ambulance!	Chame uma ambulância!	shahm'oo-muh añ-boo-**lañ**-see-uh
Call the police!	Chame a polícia!	shahm'uh poo-**lee**-see-uh
Call the fire brigade!	Chame os bombeiros!	shahm'oosh bom-**bay**-roosh
Where is the nearest telephone?	Há um telefone aqui perto?	ah ooñ te-le-**fon'**uh **keepehr**-too
Where is the nearest hospital?	Onde é o hospital mais próximo?	ond'**eh** oo ohsh-pee-**tahl'**mysh **pro**-see-moo

COMMUNICATION ESSENTIALS

Yes	Sim	seeñ
No	Não	nowñ
Please	Por favor/ Faz favor	poor fuh-**vor** fash **fuh**-vor
Thank you	Obrigado/da	o-bree-**gah**-doo/duh
Excuse me	Desculpe	dish-**koolp'**
Hello	Olá	oh-**lah**
Goodbye	Adeus	a-**deh**-oosh
Good morning	Bom-dia	boñ dee-uh
Yesterday	Ontem	oñ-**tayñ**
Today	Hoje	ohj'
Tomorrow	Amanhã	ah-mañ-**yañ**
Here	Aqui	uh-**kee**
There	Ali	uh-**lee**
What?	O quê?	oo keh
Which?	Qual?	kwahl'
When?	Quando?	kwañ-doo
Why?	Porquê?	poor-**keh**
Where?	Onde?	oñd'

USEFUL PHRASES

How are you?	Como está?	koh-moo shtah
Very well, thank you.	Bem, obrigado/da.	bayñ o-bree-**gah**-doo/duh

Pleased to meet you.	Encantado /a.	eñ-kañ-**tah**-doo/duh
See you soon.	Até logo.	uh-**teh loh**-goo
That's fine.	Está bem.	shtah bayñ
Where is/ are ...?	Onde está/ estão ... ?	ond'shtah/ shtowñ
How far is it to ...?	A que distância fica ... ?	uh kee dish-tañ-see-uh **fee**-kuh
Which way to ...?	Como se vai para ... ?	koh-moo seh vy puh-ruh
Do you speak English?	Fala inglês?	fah-luh eeñ-glehsh
I don't understand.	Não. compreendo	nowñ kom-pree-**eñ**-doo
Could you speak more slowly please?	Pode falar mais devagar por favor?	pohd'fuh-lar mysh d'-va-gar poor fuh-**vor**
I'm sorry.	Desculpe.	dish-**koolp'**

USEFUL WORDS

big	grande	grañd'
small	pequeno	pe-keh-noo
hot	quente	keñt'
cold	frio	free-oo
good	bom	boñ
bad	mau	mah-oo
quite a lot/ enough	bastante	bash-tañt'
well	bem	bayñ
open	aberto	a-behr-too
closed	fechado	fe-shah-doo
left	esquerda	shkehr-duh
right	direita	dee-ray-tuh
straight on	em frente	ayñ freñt'
near	perto	pehr-too
far	longe	loñj'
up	para cima	pur-ruh see-muh
down	para baixo	pur-ruh buy-shoo
early	cedo	seh-doo
late	tarde	tard'
entrance	entrada	eñ-trah-duh
exit	saída	sa-ee-duh
toilets	casa de banho	kah-zuh d' bañ-yoo
more	mais	mysh
less	menos	meh-noosh

MAKING A TELEPHONE CALL

I'd like to place an international call.	Queria fazer uma chamada internacional.	kree-uh fuh-**zehr** oo-muh sha-**mah**-duh in-ter-na-**see**-oo-nahl'
a local call.	uma chamada local.	oo-muh sha-**mah**-duh loo-**kahl**'
Can I leave a message?	Posso deixar uma mensagem?	poh-soo day-**shar** oo-muh meñ-**sah**-jayñ

SHOPPING

How much does this cost?	Quanto custa isto?	kwañ-too koosh-tuh eesh-too
I would like ...	Queria ...	kree-uh
I'm just looking.	Estou só a ver obrigado/a.	shtoh sohuh vehr o-bree-gah-doo/uh
Do you take credit cards?	Aceita cartões de crédito?	uh-**say**-tuh kar-**toinsh** de **kreh**-dee-too
What time do you open?	A que horas abre?	uh kee oh-rash ah-bre
What time do you close?	A que horas fecha?	uh kee oñ-rash fay-shuh
This one	Este	ehst'
That one	Esse	ehss'
expensive	caro	**kah**-roo
cheap	barato	buh-**rah**-too
size (clothes/shoes)	tamanho	ta-**man**-yoo
white	branco	**brañ**-koo
black	preto	**preh**-too
red	vermelho	ver-**mehl**'-yoo
yellow	amarelo	uh-muh-**reh**-loo
green	verde	**vehrd**'
blue	azul	uh-**zool**'

TYPES OF SHOP

antique shop	loja de antiguidades	**loh**-juh de añ-tee-gwee-**dahd**'sh
bakery	padaria	pah-duh-**ree**-uh
bank	banco	**bañ**-koo
bookshop	livraria	lee-vruh-**ree**-uh
butcher	talho	**tah**-lyoo

cake shop	pastelaria	posh-te-luh-**ree**-uh
chemist	farmácia	far-**mah**-see-uh
fishmonger	peixaria	pay-shuh-**ree**-uh
hairdresser	cabeleireiro	kab'-lay-ray-roo
market	mercado	mehr-**kah**-doo
newsagent	quiosque	kee-**yohsk**'
post office	correios	koo-**ray**-oosh
shoe shop	sapataria	suh-puh-tuh-**ree**-uh
supermarket	supermercado	soo-pehr-mer-**kah**-doo
tobacconist	tabacaria	tuh-buh-kuh-**ree**-uh
travel agency	agência de viagens	uh-**jen**-see-uh de vee-ah-jayñsh

SIGHTSEEING

cathedral	sé	seh
church	igreja	ee-**gray**-juh
garden	jardim	jar-**deeñ**
library	biblioteca	bee-blee-oo-**teh**-kuh
museum	museu	moo-**zeh**-oo
tourist information office	posto de turismo	**posh**-too d' too-**reesh**-moo
closed for holidays	fechado para férias	fe-**sha**-doo puh-ruh **feh**-ree-ash
bus station	estação de autocarros	shta-**sowñ** d' oh-too-**kah**-roosh
railway station	estação de comboios	shta-**sowñ** d' koñ-**boy**-oosh

EATING OUT

Have you got a table for...?	Tem uma mesa para ...?	tayñ oo-muh **meh**-zuh puh-ruh
I want to reserve a table.	Quero reservar uma mesa.	**keh**-roo re-zehr-**var** oo-muh **meh**-zuh
The bill please.	A conta por favor/ faz favor.	uh **kohn**-tuh poor fuh-**vor**/fash fuh-**vor**

I am a vegetarian.	**Sou vegetariano /a.**	*Soh ve-je-tuh-ree-ah-noo/ uh*	11	**onze**	*oñz'*
			12	**doze**	*doz'*
Waiter!	**Por favor!/ Faz favor!**	*poor fuh-vor/ fash fuh-vor*	13	**treze**	*trez'*
			14	**catorze**	*ka-torz'*
the menu	**a lista**	*uh **leesh**-tuh*	15	**quinze**	*keeñz'*
fixed-price menu	**a ementa turística**	*uh ee-**mehñ**-tuh too-**reesh**-tee-kuh*	16	**dezasseis**	*de-zuh-saysh*
			17	**dezassete**	*de-zuh-**set'***
wine list	**a lista de vinhos**	*uh **leesh**-tuh de **veeñ**-yoosh*	18	**dezoito**	*de-**zoy**-too*
			19	**dezanove**	*de-zuh-**nov'***
			20	**vinte**	*veent'*
breakfast	**pequeno-almoço**	*pe-**keh**-noo-ahl-**moh**-soo*	21	**vinte e um**	*veen-tee-ooñ*
			30	**trinta**	*treeñ-tuh*
lunch	**almoço**	*ahl-**moh**-soo*	40	**quarenta**	*kwa-reñ-tuh*
dinner	**jantar**	*jan-**tar***	50	**cinquenta**	*seen-**kweñ**-tuh*
cover	**couvert**	*koo-**vehr***	60	**sessenta**	*se-**señ**-tuh*
starter	**entrada**	*eñ-**trah**-duh*	70	**setenta**	*se-**teñ**-tuh*
main course	**prato principal**	*prah-too prin--see-pahl'*	80	**oitenta**	*oy-**teñ**-tuh*
			90	**noventa**	*noo-**veñ**-tuh*
			100	**cem**	*sayñ*
dish of the day	**prato do dia**	*prah-too doo dee-uh*	101	**cento e um**	*señ-too-ee-ooñ*
dessert	**sobremesa**	*soh-bre-**meh**-zuh*	102	**cento e dois**	*señ-too ee doysh*
			200	**duzentos**	*doo-**zeñ**-toosh*
NUMBERS			300	**trezentos**	*tre-**zeñ**-toosh*
0	**zero**	*zeh-roo*	400	**quatrocentos**	*kwa-troo-**señ**-toosh*
1	**um**	*ooñ*			
2	**dois**	*doysh*	500	**quinhentos**	*kee-**nyeñ**-toosh*
3	**três**	*tresh*			
4	**quatro**	*kwa-troo*	700	**setecentos**	*set'-**señ**-toosh*
5	**cinco**	*seeñ-koo*			
6	**seis**	*saysh*	900	**novecentos**	*nov'-**señ**-toosh*
7	**sete**	*set'*			
8	**oito**	*oy-too*	1,000	**mil**	*meel'*
9	**nove**	*nov'*			
10	**dez**	*desh*			